THE CHRONICLE OF
WESTERN COSTUME

JOHN PEACOCK

THE CHRONICLE OF

COMPLETE IN COLOUR WITH MORE THAN 1000 ILLUSTRATIONS

WESTERN COSTUME

From the Ancient World to the late Twentieth Century

THAMES AND HUDSON

For Kimberley

Contents

Preface

THIS CHRONICLE OF COSTUME STYLES covers roughly four thousand years of history and several cultures. My purpose in researching and compiling the book has been to create an accessible visual chronology of the mainstream development of Western costume. For the sake of historical completeness the survey begins in the Eastern Mediterranean and includes examples from the Egyptian and Mesopotamian cultures and, in those sections concerned with the late-nineteenth and twentieth centuries, source material from the United States of America has also been added. *The Chronicle* is not intended to be an academic study of the history of Western costume. On the whole, I have tended to avoid costume styles deriving from ethnic or nationalistic dress, even when they have been transformed from peasant costume into 'high fashion' as was the case, for instance, with the various types of Austro-Hungarian court dress, which incorporated elements of folk costume. In several instances I have simplified the drawings in order to trace the development of certain styles. Occasionally I have amalgamated parts from various sources in order to show a complete costume. Although *The Chronicle* is mainly concerned with middle- and upper-class costume styles, some examples of clothes worn by the working class have been included for purposes of comparison.

Within such a long time span some problems of terminology and classification have obviously arisen. For those archaic, but historically accurate, expressions which may cause confusion to the non-specialist, I have substituted modern terms which today's reader may more easily understand. Though I am well aware of the dangers of oversimplification, I have followed this practice particularly in writing about colour, fabric, foundation garments and regional or national variations of the same basic costume type. For example, I have opted to describe as a sacque the very familiar ladies' dress of the mid-eighteenth century known in its various manifestations as a Watteau back, a sac, a sacque, a sack back, a trollopee, a robe à la française, a robe à l'anglaise and, when gathered up round the skirts, as a polonaise. Elsewhere similar simplifications have been undertaken.

Descriptions of fabric are equally fraught with danger. Some terms used in the past are quite straightforward technical words which have retained the same meaning today, whilst others are fashionable descriptions of a cloth which we may know as something else or which we may be unable to identify at all. Brocade, velvet, taffeta and satin are all comprehensible words to today's reader. However, caffoy, harateen, lutestring and moreen are not only obscure as terms but also in some cases the fabrics are not clearly identifiable, even by costume historians. Colour terminology is subject to the same changes of fashion and usage, as anyone consulting a modern paint-chart will quickly realize. Thus I have avoided the terms Cheruse, Nottingham, Bougival or flake, for instance, in favour of the rather more accessible 'white'.

The illustrated glossary provides an explanation of descriptive or technical terms which the non-specialist may encounter in the book. A brief bibliography is also appended. As the works included have been useful to me in compiling this survey, I can recommend them to others wishing to extend their knowledge and undertake further research.

JOHN PEACOCK

ANCIENT EGYPT c. 2000-1700 bc

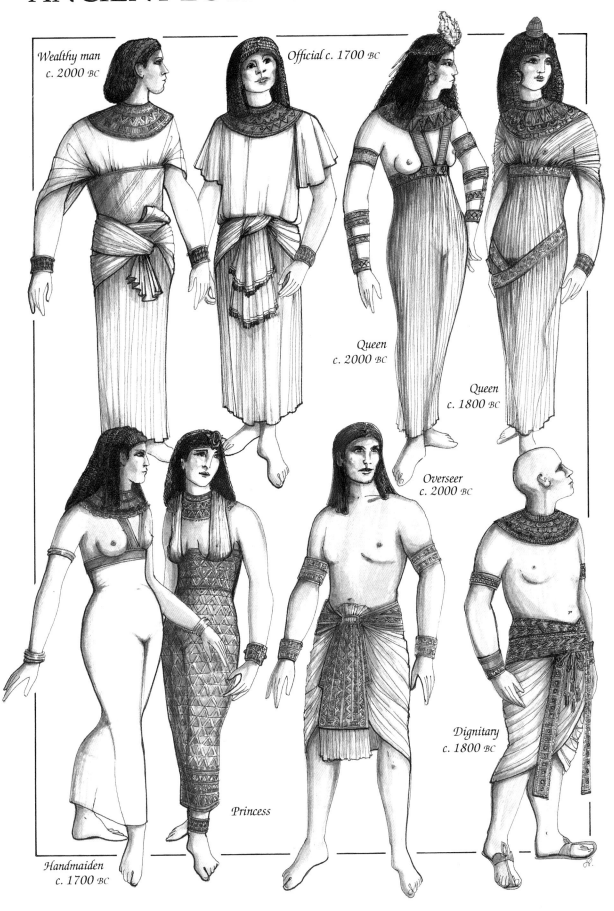

Wealthy man
c. 2000 bc

Official c. 1700 bc

Queen
c. 2000 bc

Queen
c. 1800 bc

Overseer
c. 2000 bc

Dignitary
c. 1800 bc

Princess

Handmaiden
c. 1700 bc

ANCIENT EGYPT c. 1500-1200 BC

Scribe c. 1500 BC

Wealthy woman
c. 1450 BC

Princess c. 1300 BC

Priestess
c. 1300 BC

Man-servant
c. 1420 BC

Working man
c. 1500–1200 BC

Prince
c. 1490 BC

Guard c. 1200 BC

ANCIENT EGYPT C. 1500-1200 BC

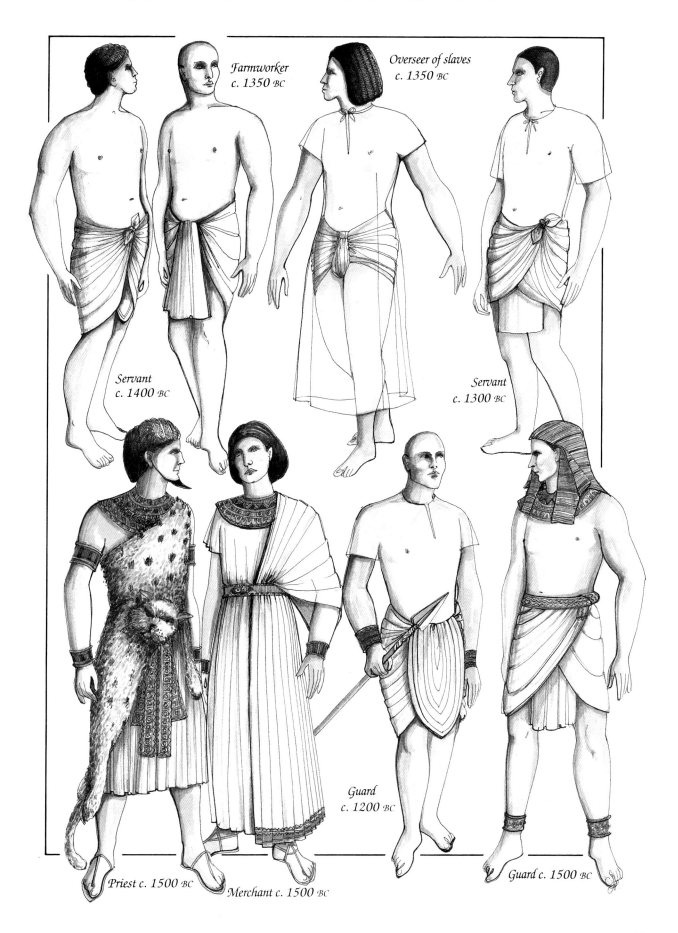

Farmworker
c. 1350 BC

Overseer of slaves
c. 1350 BC

Servant
c. 1400 BC

Servant
c. 1300 BC

Guard
c. 1200 BC

Priest c. 1500 BC

Merchant c. 1500 BC

Guard c. 1500 BC

ANCIENT CRETE c. 2000-1200 BC

Goddess

Princess

King

Soldier

Working woman

Working man

Wealthy woman

Athlete

Servant

ANCIENT GREECE c. 600-480 BC

Woman
c. 600–480 BC

Young man
c. 600 BC

Lady
c. 600–480 BC

Traveller
c. 500 BC

Woman c. 500 BC

Woman c. 500 BC

Woman c. 500 BC

Woman c. 540 BC

Orator c. 500 BC

ANCIENT GREECE c. 480-450 BC

Attendant
c. 480 BC

Lady c. 480 BC

Man
c. 470–450 BC

Woman
c. 470–450 BC

Warrior
c. 460 BC

Warrior
c. 460 BC

Maid-servant
c. 450 BC

Lady c. 460 BC

14

ANCIENT GREECE C. 440-400 BC

Woman c. 440 BC

Lady c. 440 BC

Matron c. 420 BC

Priestess c. 420 BC

Dancer c. 400 BC

Guard c. 400 BC

Man c. 400 BC

Warrior c. 440 BC

15

ANCIENT GREECE c. 300-150 bc

Working man
c. 300–150 bc

Household servant
c. 300–150 bc

Lady c. 300 bc

Woman
c. 200 bc

Woman c. 190 bc

Traveller c. 150 bc

Matron c. 250 bc

Charioteer c. 150 bc

BABYLON AND ASSYRIA C. 1200-500 BC

Babylonian king c. 1200 BC

Assyrian nobleman c. 1200 BC

Nobleman c. 880 BC

Priest c. 870 BC

Babylonian woman c. 1100 BC

Nobleman c. 700 BC

Assyrian queen c. 500 BC

Assyrian queen c. 800 BC

ASSYRIA C. 750 BC-100 AD

Soldier
c. 750 BC

Guard
c. 650 BC

Nobleman
c. 600 BC

Hunter
c. 620 BC

High priest
c. 200 BC

Commoner
c. 700 BC—100 AD

Attendant c. 200 BC

Nobleman c. 100 AD

PERSIA c. 600-500 BC

Working man

Maid-servant

Prince

Queen

Servant

Nobleman

Soldier

King

ANCIENT ROME c. 750-300 BC

Working man
c. 750–300 BC

Men c. 750 BC

Gymnast
c. 400
–300 BC

Dancing girl
c. 500 BC

Working man
c. 750–300 BC

Gladiator c. 300 BC

Servant c. 300 BC

Shepherd c. 350 BC

Wealthy man c. 300 BC

ANCIENT ROME c. 100 BC-25 AD

Lady c. 100 BC

Lady c. 100 BC

Traveller c. 50 BC

Lady c. 50 BC

Grand lady
c. 25 AD

Senator c. 25 AD

Traveller c. 25 AD

Lady c. 25 AD

ANCIENT ROME C. 50-200 AD

Grand lady
c. 50–150 AD

Senator's wife
c. 150–200 AD

Man of royal blood
c. 200 AD

Grand lady
c. 50–150 AD

Soldier c. 150 AD

Guard c. 138 AD

Centurion c. 150 AD

Priest c. 150–200 AD

ANCIENT ROME c. 200-487 AD

Traveller
c. 200 AD

Soldier c. 200 AD

Guard
c. 230 AD

Serving girl
c. 200–250 AD

Members of the Senate c. 300–487 AD

BYZANTIUM C. 500-1200 AD

Soldier c. 500 AD

Lady c. 500 AD

Commoner c. 500–800 AD

Empress c. 500 AD

Courtier c. 600 AD

Priest c. 600 AD

Princess c. 1100 AD

Emperor c. 1200 AD

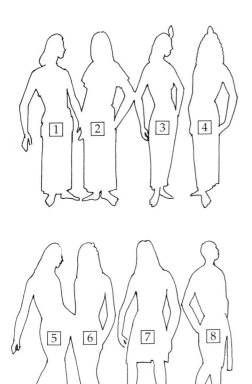

ANCIENT EGYPT C. 2000–1700 BC

1 Wealthy man *c.* 2000 BC: linen wig; painted collar; wide quilted belt; fine hip-girdle. 2 Official *c.* 1700 BC: painted collar; white linen robe; knotted waist-sash; bracelets. 3 Queen *c.* 2000 BC: long curled wig with plume; finely pleated robe falling from under the bust; geometric patterned armbands. 4 Queen *c.* 1800 BC: large wig topped with wax cone of perfume; pleated linen robe wrapped in cape effect; belt under the bust and around the hips.

5 Handmaiden *c.* 1700 BC: long tubular robe with high belt and straps between the breasts; gold and brightly coloured collar of beads. 6 Princess *c.* 1700 BC: long curled and oiled wig decorated with lotus-flower brooch; ankle-length, tubular robe; transparent linen covering the breasts. 7 Overseer *c.* 2000 BC: loincloth draped to the knees; painted hip-belt and sash; gold and enamel armbands and bracelets. 8 Dignitary *c.* 1800 BC: shaved head; collar and armlets of gold and beads; wide hip-sash decorated with embroidery and beads; swathed loincloth.

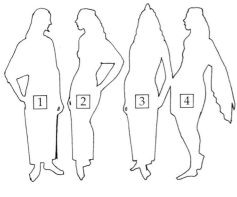

ANCIENT EGYPT C. 1500–1200 BC

1 Scribe *c.* 1500 BC: long wig and false beard; brightly coloured collar and armlets; transparent linen robe with hip-sash; sandals. 2 Wealthy woman *c.* 1450 BC: headdress of gold and enamel; matching collar; large earrings; transparent linen robe knotted above the bust. 3 Princess *c.* 1300 BC: perfumed cone and curled wig; separate cape top; pleated ankle-length skirt with narrow belt under the bust. 4 Priestess *c.* 1300 BC: gold headdress; spiral earrings; draped robe of transparent white linen, knotted at the waist.

5 Man-servant *c.* 1420 BC: wide collar over T-shaped shift; belt; short loincloth. 6 Working man *c.* 1500–1200 BC: close-fitting short wig; pleated loincloth with sash; knee-length, fine linen overshift. 7 Prince *c.* 1490 BC: cloth-covered wig; gold fillet; false beard; stylized loincloth of gold and enamel over simple linen loincloth. 8 Guard *c.* 1200 BC: linen robe; draped sash and belt; wide leather belt from chest to hip.

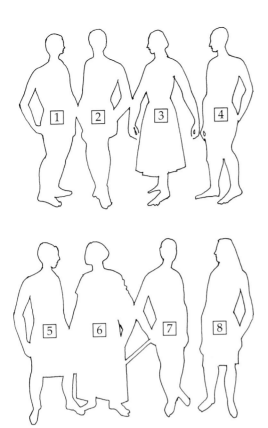

ANCIENT EGYPT C. 1500–1200 BC

1 Servant *c.* 1400 BC: closely curled wig; knee-length draped loincloth knotted low at the front. 2 Farmworker *c.* 1350 BC: shaved head; short, white linen loincloth draped and folded at the front. 3 Overseer of slaves *c.* 1350 BC: chin-length, thick linen wig; small draped loincloth under ankle-length, transparent linen tunic. 4 Servant *c.* 1300 BC: felt cap cut around the ears; short transparent shirt tucked into draped loincloth.

5 Priest *c.* 1500 BC: short black wig; false beard; gold and enamel collar, armlets and bracelets; knee-length skirt and decorative gold loincloth under animal-skin mantle; fine sandals. 6 Merchant *c.* 1500 BC: elaborate beaded collar over ankle-length robe with decorative border; mantle draped over one shoulder and held in place with gold belt; sandals. 7 Guard *c.* 1200 BC: shaved head; transparent linen shirt; loincloth; bracelets. 8 Guard *c.* 1500 BC: brightly coloured cloth wig in woven stripes; painted collar, anklets and belt holding draped loincloth.

ANCIENT CRETE C. 2000–1200 BC

1 Goddess: gold crown; long hair in ringlets; bodice with elbow-length sleeves, cut away under the bust; narrow tight-fitting belt at the waist; decorative apron; bell-shaped skirt. 2 Princess: gold and enamel headband; necklace of tiny beads; embroidered bodice; padded belt; bell-shaped skirt falling to the ground. 3 King: jewelled crown with long feather; necklace of beads and shells; solid belt encircling the waist; embroidered short loincloth leading to tassel at the front; short leather boots. 4 Soldier: decorated metal helmet topped with long feathers; embroidered, long-sleeved leather tunic split at the sides; footless gaiters.

5 Working woman: T-shaped, ankle-length robe of coarse linen; wide leather belt. 6 Working man: long hair and pointed beard; T-shaped linen tunic with decorative coloured bands; waist-belt. 7 Wealthy woman: close-fitting, front-laced bodice decorated with beads and embroidery; tight belt; divided skirt. 8 Athlete: linen loincloth; tight belt; leather bracelets. 9 Servant: short tunic with bound edges and seams; leather belt.

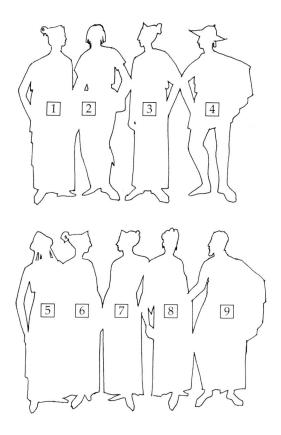

ANCIENT GREECE C. 600–480 BC

1. Woman c. 600–480 BC: hair arranged in tight curls with wide beaded headband; open-sided gown with overfold to the waist, held at each shoulder with pins. 2. Young man c. 600 BC: hair dressed into ringlets with narrow headband; short T-shaped tunic; wide leather belt; knee-length, soft leather boots. 3. Lady c. 600–480 BC: elaborate fillet; curled hair; drop earrings; chiton with draped overfolds under the bust and over the hips, slit at the sides and pinned at the shoulders. 4. Traveller c. 500 BC: wide-brimmed hat; short circular-cut cloak with narrow border; leg bindings; soft leather shoes.

5. Woman c. 500 BC: gown with decorative border at the centre front and around the hem; belt under the bust; shawl draped over one shoulder; flat leather sandals. 6. Woman c. 500 BC: tunic with overfold to hip level, belted tightly at the waist, with deep border of yellow, orange and blue stripes and fringed edge. 7. Woman c. 500 BC: hair dressed over and around wide headband; necklace of beads; tunic with dark-blue and red overfold; leather shoes. 8. Woman c. 540 BC: tunic with dark-blue and red overfold in bold geometric patterns. 9. Orator c. 500 BC: beard; long hair; leather fillet; robe draped over one shoulder; leather sandals.

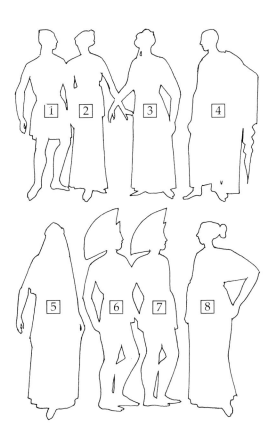

ANCIENT GREECE C. 480–450 BC

1. Attendant c. 480 BC: skull cap; patterned tunic; waist-belt with geometric design; sandals. 2. Lady c. 480 BC: bound headscarf; necklace of tiny shells; chiton with overfold to hip and patterned panel at centre front; sash under the bust. 3. Woman c. 470–450 BC: chiton pinned at the shoulders with front drapery and deep border at hem; waist-belt. 4. Man c. 470–450 BC: short hair combed forward and held with fillet; bordered robe thrown over one shoulder.

5. Lady c. 460 BC: tiara with enamel decoration; hip-length veil; earrings; fine cotton chiton with overfold dipping to the back, the border in blue and orange strips. 6. 7. Warriors c. 460 BC: metal helmets with visors and neck shields; plumes of horsehair dyed red; metal breastplates and shoulder-guards; short skirts; leg armour. 8. Maid-servant c. 450 BC: elaborate hairstyle secured with scarf and fillet; white linen tunic with wide patterned border.

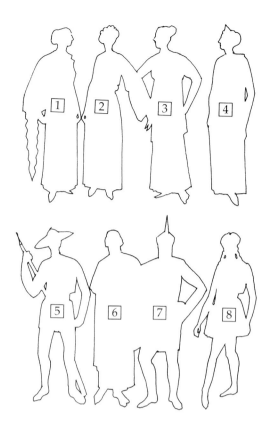

ANCIENT GREECE C. 440–400 BC

1 Lady c. 440 BC: embroidered and beaded cap; gold wire earrings; elaborately arranged chiton with narrow border. 2 Priestess c. 420 BC: hair dressed away from the face and decorated with wreath of gold flowers; simple chiton of white linen with folds and pleats. 3 Woman c. 440 BC: hair arranged in curls and ringlets; chiton with two overfolds, held under the bust and over the shoulders with ribbon binding. 4 Matron c. 420 BC: gold tiara and earrings; fabric cap secured with narrow fillet; chiton with short overfold and shoulder pins.

5 Guard c. 400 BC: metal helmet with wide brim; thigh-length tunic of brightly coloured linen outlined in strong geometric borders. 6 Man c. 400 BC: ankle-length tunic; draped shawl with deep border of stylized flowers and leaves. 7 Warrior c. 440 BC: metal helmet with neck shield, spike and adjustable visor; short tunic; overskirt in brightly coloured linen. 8 Dancer c. 400 BC: long curled hair; semi-transparent, knee-length pleated tunic pinned on to one shoulder and bound at the waist.

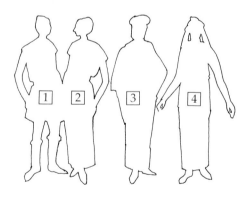

ANCIENT GREECE C. 300–150 BC

1 Working man c. 300–150 BC: short cropped hair; skull cap; tunic of coarse linen or wool to mid-thigh; leather leg protection up to the knee; coarse leather shoes. 2 Household servant c. 300–150 BC: linen cap held in place by narrow leather fillet; rough shift. 3 Lady c. 300 BC: disc-shaped straw sunhat; stole bound tightly around the body; straw fan. 4 Woman c. 200 BC: tiara with long veil attached at the back; chiton with wide decorative border and uneven overfold from under the bust.

5 Matron c. 250 BC: necklace; long chiton covered by bright-orange shawl; leather mules. 6 Charioteer c. 150 BC: short hair; gold fillet; short circular-cut cloak; knee-length tunic with short sleeves and painted and embroidered decoration; sandals. 7 Woman c. 190 BC: gold tiara and hair decoration; chiton and overfold to hips; cross-over belt and straps of narrow ribbon. 8 Traveller c. 150 BC: dark-red tunic falling to the ankles; stole with deep border bound tightly around the body and over the head.

BABYLON AND ASSYRIA C. 1200–500 BC

1 Babylonian king c. 1200 BC: tall gold crown decorated with feathers; embroidered robe with apron front; wide belt; straps crossing the chest. 2 Assyrian nobleman c. 1200 BC: fillet of gold leaves worn over long hair; shawl with gold tassel fringe; shoes. 3 Nobleman c. 880 BC: truncated hat; long hair and beard dressed into ringlets; short tunic with bound hem; rich yellow shawl with fringe; silk sash. 4 Priest c. 870 BC: long hair and beard; short tunic with fringed hem; shawl pinned on to one shoulder.

5 Assyrian queen c. 800 BC: gold crown and earrings; woven patterned shawl embroidered at the edges and adorned with tassel fringe. 6 Babylonian woman c. 1100 BC: white stole with bands of bright colour bordering the edges; leather mules. 7 Assyrian queen c. 500 BC: tunic patterned with bands of geometric embroidery; fringed shawl; heavy bangles. 8 Nobleman c. 700 BC: tall truncated hat; long hair and beard; embroidered robe; wool shawl with tassel fringe; shoes.

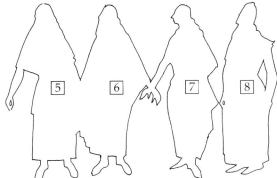

ASSYRIA C. 750 BC–100 AD

1 Soldier c. 750 BC: metal helmet with chin strap; long hair and beard; wide, stiff leather belt worn over red tunic; breeches; stockings; boots. 2 Guard c. 650 BC: helmet with single feather plume; wool tunic; cross-over straps on chest; wide waist-belt. 3 Nobleman c. 600 BC: truncated hat; long hair and beard; bead necklace; skirt with fringed hem; wide belt; leather armlets; red leather boots. 4 Hunter c. 620 BC: leather headband, wristlets and belt; draped skirt with fringing; sandals.

5 High priest c. 200 BC: headdress with shallow crown; stiff bodice; belt with flower motif echoed in bracelets; skirt with fringing. 6 Attendant c. 200 BC: short bodice and separate skirt; woven, fringed shawl; feather fan. 7 Commoner c. 700 BC–100 AD: short hair and beard; T-shaped tunic; leather thong belt. 8 Nobleman c. 100 AD: tunic with separate skirt; shawl with gold embroidery and fringing.

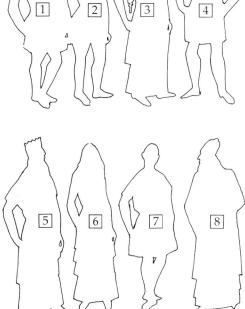

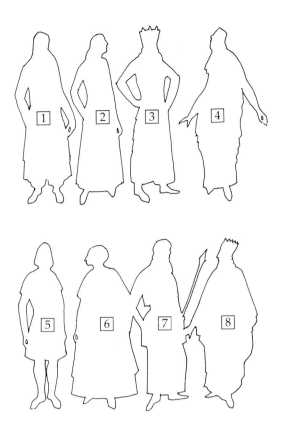

PERSIA C. 600–500 BC

1 Working man: fabric cap with chin straps; tunic with belt under full coat; trousers; shoes. 2 Maid-servant: hair drawn back under headband; chemise with long sleeves, decorated on the upper arms and around the neck. 3 Prince: tall crown embellished with feathers and brooches; decorated, wide leather belt; trousers tied at the ankle. 4 Queen: headdress with gold discs; gold earrings and necklace; shawl and skirt with tassled fringe.

5 Servant: T-shaped linen tunic falling to the knees; small mantle draped over one shoulder. 6 Nobleman: swathed hat; large coat of woven, striped wool with fringing, held at the front with brooches and beads; underrobe with deep fringe hem. 7 Soldier: all-leather cap; tunic worn over trousers; boots. 8 King: tall gold crown; embroidered robe with long sleeves; boots.

ANCIENT ROME C. 750–300 BC

1 Working man *c.* 750–300 BC: mid-thigh-length tunic draped over one shoulder and belted at the waist; leather ankle-boots. 2 Working man *c.* 750–300 BC: T-shaped, knee-length tunic; sandals. 3 4 Men *c.* 750 BC: short hair combed forward; toga with coloured borders, placed over one shoulder and arranged into folds; leather sandals. 5 Gymnast *c.* 400–300 BC: fabric bound around the bust; brief pants. 6 Dancing girl *c.* 500 BC: elaborately coiled hair; high-waisted robe; long stole of fine transparent fabric.

7 Gladiator *c.* 300 BC: asymmetric tunic with skirt folded to form shorts; wide leather belt; one arm protected with padded and studded leather, the other with shield; ankle-boots. 8 Servant *c.* 300 BC: shift of lightweight linen slit at the arms. 9 Shepherd *c.* 350 BC: wide-brimmed straw hat; coarse leather cape tied on one shoulder; sheepskin tunic; knee-high boots. 10 Wealthy man *c.* 300 BC: fillet of gold leaves; large stole with wide border of leaves and flowers; sandals.

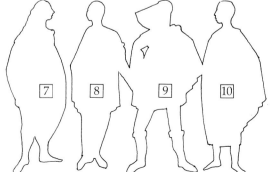

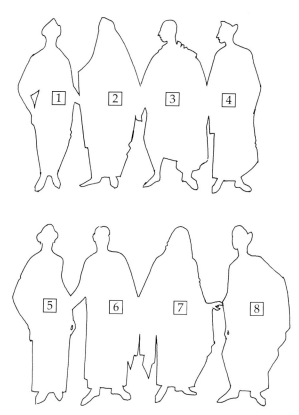

ANCIENT ROME C. 100 BC–25 AD

[1] Lady c. 100 BC: gold tiara; pale-cream robe; pale-green silk stole; sandals with thick soles. [2] Lady c. 100 BC: enamel and gold tiara; long, purple silk veil over cream robe; mules. [3] Traveller c. 50 BC: long cloak with overcape, fastened at the front with clasp; short tunic with deep hem border; leg bindings; ankle-boots. [4] Lady c. 50 BC: hair dressed into tiara shape; long shawl with deep border, draped over pale-blue robe.

[5] Grand lady c. 25 AD: gold tiara, earrings and necklace; robe worn over ankle-length chemise with pinned sleeves. [6] Senator c. 25 AD: short hair; toga draped over ankle-length underrobe; laced boots with open toes. [7] Traveller c. 25 AD: full chemise; long stole wound around the body and over the head; sandals. [8] Lady c. 25 AD: elaborately dressed hair; long chemise with waist cord; long, pale-green silk stole.

ANCIENT ROME C. 50–200 AD

[1] Grand lady c. 50–150 AD: large tiara; hair curled high on the forehead; shawl with bright-red border, wrapped around ankle-length chemise. [2] Grand lady c. 50–150 AD: pale-green silk chemise under shorter cream robe; asymmetric stole. [3] Senator's wife c. 150–200 AD: gold earrings; stole; chemise. [4] Man of royal blood c. 200 AD: gold fillet; chemise; purple toga; sandals.

[5] Soldier c. 150 AD: helmet with single red plume; short circular cape pinned at shoulder; knee-length skirt; belt over leather breastplate; wristlets; sturdy sandals. [6] Guard c. 138 AD: helmet with visor and tall plumed crest; metal and leather armour; leather ankle-boots with open front. [7] Centurion c. 150 AD: plumed helmet; cape; leather armour worn over red wool undertunic and short breeches; red leather boots. [8] Priest c. 150–200 AD: large toga with purple border, drawn around the body and over the head.

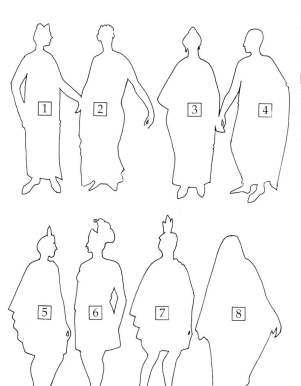

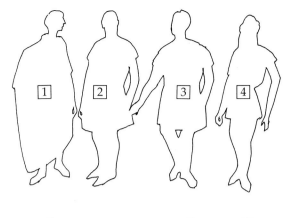

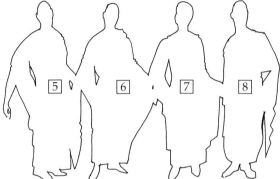

ANCIENT ROME C. 200–487 AD

1 Traveller c. 200 AD: cropped hair; full circular cloak; short tunic over knee-breeches; long boots. 2 Soldier c. 200 AD: shiny metal breastplate with engraved pattern of flowers and leaves; fringed leather sleeves and overskirt; red wool undertunic; long embroidered boots. 3 Guard c. 230 AD: metal helmet with visor and neck shield; wide shoulder-pads of leather and metal; moulded breastplates; red wool undertunic; open sandals. 4 Serving girl c. 200–250 AD: lightweight wool tunic falling to mid-thigh; ribbon belt.

5 – 8 Members of the Senate c. 300–487 AD: togas of differing lengths and widths, with and without borders, bound and draped in styles of varying complexity.

BYZANTIUM C. 500–1200 AD

1 Soldier c. 500 AD: metal helmet; circular cape; patterned breastplate, belt and armlets; knee-length tunic; stockings bound with leather. 2 Lady c. 500 AD: large turban; gold earrings and necklace; belt decorated with precious stones; lilac chemise; light-brown overtunic; pink stole. 3 Commoner c. 500–800 AD: felt hat; T-shaped robe; long wool stole with geometric patterned border. 4 Empress c. 500 AD: crown set with gems; embroidered collar and stole decorated with jewels; simple tunic with jewelled hem; red leather shoes.

5 Courtier c. 600 AD: T-shaped tunic with brightly coloured embroidery; long green cloak with decorated panels and borders; open-toed knee-boots laced up the front. 6 Priest c. 600 AD: green oval cape; purple tunic with decorated edges; long stole.
7 Princess c. 1100 AD: large crown, earrings, bracelets and gold belt set with precious stones; green chemise; knee-length overtunic.
8 Emperor c. 1200 AD: large crown; wide collar, tunic and chemise of richly woven silk re-embroidered with gold threads and set with gems.

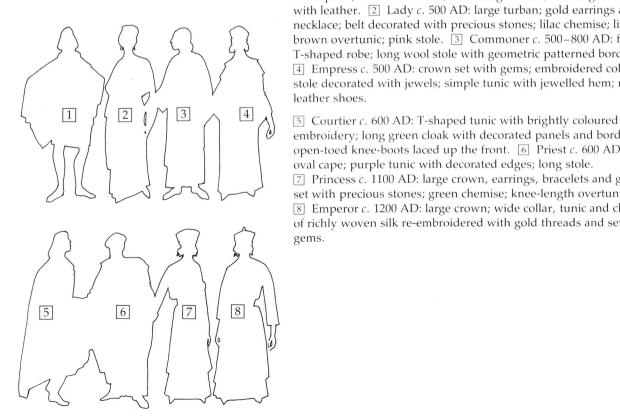

c. 100-950 AD

Teutonic warrior
c. 100–900 AD

Spanish
working man
c. 500–600 AD

Monk c. 600 AD

Danish women c. 600-800 AD

Spanish lady c. 650–700 AD

Frenchwoman
c. 850 AD

French king c. 845 AD

Frenchman c. 850 AD

Anglo-Saxon
nobleman
c. 950 AD

C. 950-1100

Traveller
c. 950

English soldier
c. 950

French soldier
c. 950

Frenchwoman c. 1000

German woman
c. 1095

Englishwoman c. 1084

Bohemian king c. 1085

English lady c. 1087

German nobleman c. 1100

c. 1100-1115

English country worker c. 1100–1115

English country worker c. 1100–1115

English nobleman c. 1100

French queen c. 1100

French cleric c. 1110

Bishop c. 1110

French countrywoman c. 1100–1115

English gentleman c. 1100

Frenchman c. 1115

c. 1120-1150

German woman c. 1120–1150

German lady c. 1130

English shepherd c. 1120–1150

French rustic c. 1150

German lady c. 1150

French lady c. 1145–1150

English queen c. 1150

German woman c. 1130–1150

French soldier c. 1150

German lady c. 1150

C. 1160-1185

Spaniard c. 1160

Italian lady c. 1160

French farmworker c. 1160

Frenchman c. 1160–1165

Englishman c. 1165

Englishwoman c. 1170

English gentleman c. 1185

Frenchwoman c. 1170

French lady c. 1185

c. 1190-1200

English lady
c. 1190

German
nobleman
c. 1190–1195

English queen
c. 1190

German nobleman
c. 1190–1195

Englishman c. 1190

English king c. 1195

French king c. 1200

Pilgrim c. 1200

C. 1200-1216

Peasant woman c. 1200

Monk of Saint Dominic c. 1200

Englishman c. 1205–1210

English lady c. 1210

Dominican nun c. 1210

German soldier c. 1200–1215

English knight c. 1216

English king c. 1215

English king c. 1216

English lady c. 1216

c. 1216-1240

Serving woman
c. 1216–1240

Italian woman
c. 1220–1230

English servant
c. 1230–1240

Crusader c. 1220

English queen
c. 1230

German noble c. 1230–1240

Working man c. 1230

English/German doctor
c. 1235–1240

c. 1240-1250

Blacksmith
c. 1240–1250

French
gentleman
c. 1245

Italian lady
c. 1240–1250

Italian tradesman
c. 1245

German girl
c. 1240–1245

Frenchman c. 1245–1250

Englishman c. 1250

German woman c. 1245

C. 1245-1260

German lady
c. 1245–1250

French soldier
c. 1245–1250

French bishop
c. 1250–1260

Frenchwoman
c. 1250

Italian lady
c. 1245–1250

Frenchman
c. 1255–1260

English lady c. 1255

French king c. 1255–1260

German gentleman c. 1250

c. 1260-1300

English nobleman
c. 1260

Englishman
c. 1260

Dutch lady
c. 1268

Shepherd
c. 1260
–1275

Shepherd c. 1260–1275

German nobleman
c. 1290

French gentleman
c. 1295–1300

French gentleman c. 1275

French lord c. 1285–1295

c. 1300-1335

English peasant
c. 1300–1335

English
farmworker
c. 1300–1335

Englishman
c. 1300–1325

English lady c. 1310

English traveller
c. 1310–1335

Countrywoman
c. 1325–1335

Young Spanish woman c. 1310–1315

Spanish lady c. 1325–1330

c. 1335-1350

Englishman
c. 1335–1340

English lord
c. 1340

Frenchman
c. 1335–1340

English farmer
c. 1335–1340

Farmworker
c. 1340

Italian merchant c. 1340

French lady c. 1340

Frenchman c. 1350

Bohemian
c. 1350

c. 1350-1369

English knight
c. 1350

English lord c. 1350

Traveller
c. 1350

Young Italian
c. 1350

Spanish lord c. 1350

German knight
c. 1369

Italian lady c. 1355–1360

English lady c. 1364

Spanish girl c. 1365

German lady c. 1369

c. 1370-1390

Italian lady c. 1370

Spanish soldier c. 1375–1385

French queen c. 1375–1378

Italian man c. 1385

Italian soldier c. 1380

Italian lady c. 1380

English lady c. 1380

Young German c. 1380–1385

Englishman c. 1385

Young German c. 1390

c. 1390-1400

Burgundian lady c. 1390

Burgundian lady c. 1390

Burgundian gentleman c. 1390

English gentleman c. 1390–1395

Young Englishman c. 1396

English scribe c. 1398

Young Frenchman c. 1393

Spanish lady c. 1395

German gentleman c. 1400

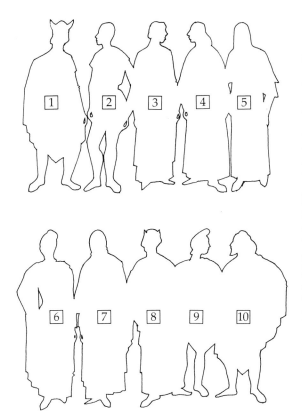

C. 100–950 AD

1 Teutonic warrior *c.* 100–900 AD: metal helmet with horns; long cloak; short tunic; wide leather belt with buckle; trousers; leg bindings. 2 Spanish working man *c.* 500–600 AD: short hair; tunic with skirt looped up to form drawers; leather belt; boots; ankle binders. 3 Monk *c.* 600 AD: partly shaven head; long tunic; tabard; leather ankle-shoes. 4 Danish woman *c.* 600–800 AD: shoulder cape of patched animal skins; ankle-length skirt with woven stripes around the hem. 5 Danish woman *c.* 600–800 AD: long dress of woven wool with part overfold; waist-belt; leather shoes.

6 Spanish lady *c.* 650–700 AD: tight-fitting, ankle-length dress with narrow sleeves; long stole. 7 Frenchwoman *c.* 850 AD: stole draped over head and shoulders; brown chemise with long sleeves worn under green mid-calf-length gown; hip-sash. 8 French king *c.* 845 AD: circular cloak; over- and undergowns; gold jewellery; leather boots. 9 Frenchman *c.* 850 AD: cap; short tunic; circular cape pinned at shoulder; leather boots. 10 Anglo-Saxon nobleman *c.* 950 AD: long hair and beard; tunic with woven, patterned bands on hem of skirt and on short sleeves.

C. 950–1100

1 Traveller *c.* 950: wide-brimmed straw sunhat; mid-calf-length overgown with hood and wide sleeves; ankle-length undergown. 2 English soldier *c.* 950: metal helmet worn over chain mail; linked metal armour to the knee; sword belt; soled chain-mail hose. 3 French soldier *c.* 950: chain-mail tunic with hood; long fabric tabard; sword belt; soled chain-mail hose. 4 Frenchwoman *c.* 1000: patterned stole worn over the head; fitted gown of red wool. 5 German woman *c.* 1095: long green wool gown with scalloped hem and wide flared sleeves with decorative edges.

6 Englishwoman *c.* 1084: short, cream linen veil; knee-length overgown with decorative borders; floor-length undergown; waist-belt. 7 Bohemian king *c.* 1085: gold crown set with precious stones; full cloak fastened with red jewelled brooch; long gown with gold embroidered borders; green hose; ankle-shoes. 8 English lady *c.* 1087: long veil and headband; full-length gown with wide bordered neckline and sleeves. 9 German nobleman *c.* 1100: cloak fastened in front with brooch; knee-length tunic; hose; leg bindings; boots.

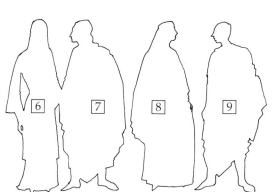

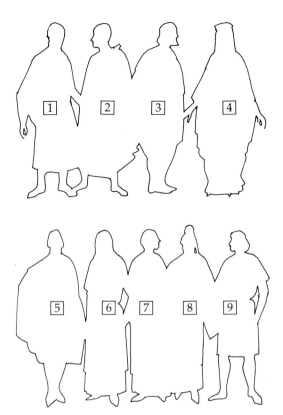

C. 1100–1115

[1] English country worker *c*. 1100–1115: shawl of coarse material; mid-calf-length grey tunic with bound hem; bound hose. [2] English country worker *c*. 1100–1115: cloak tied over one shoulder; knee-length shift; waist-belt; short hose bound with leather. [3] English nobleman *c*. 1100: short cloak with clasp on one shoulder; knee-length tunic with bound hem; red hose; leather bindings; shoes. [4] French queen *c*. 1100: crown and long veil; blue floor-length cloak with red lining and gold edging; tight-fitting, floor-length gown; hip-girdle.

[5] English gentleman *c*. 1100: knee-length cloak with shoulder cape; blue tunic; leather belt with buckle; green hose; leather shoes. [6] French countrywoman *c*. 1100–1115: veil covering head and shoulders; long gown with tight sleeves; short-sleeved tunic with band down front and around hem. [7] French cleric *c*. 1110: long gown with flared sleeves; dark-green undergown. [8] Bishop *c*. 1110: small mitre; patterned chasuble; knee-length undergown with very wide sleeves; red leather shoes. [9] Frenchman *c*. 1115: short curly hair; tunic with deep V-shaped neckline and short skirt split at the side; long leather-bound boots.

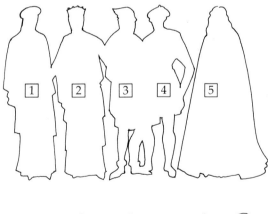

C. 1120–1150

[1] German woman *c*. 1120–1150: padded roll headdress; long veil with patterned border; overgown with flared sleeves. [2] German lady *c*. 1130: gold crown; long veil; short green overgown, the trailing sleeves trimmed with decorative edge; patterned undergown; blue chemise. [3] English shepherd *c*. 1120–1150: fur-lined hood; knee-length tunic split at the front; rolled-down ankle-boots. [4] French rustic *c*. 1150: small hat with padded brim; short tunic; leather belt; boots. [5] German lady *c*. 1150: long hair; gold fillet; floor-length cloak with fur lining; sleeveless, V-necked loose overtunic with bold geometric pattern.

[6] French lady *c*. 1145–1150: wide gold headband set with precious stones; long braided hair; gown with flared sleeves; waist-belt and hip-girdle. [7] English queen *c*. 1150: long veil falling from gold crown; floor-length gown with geometric decoration on short sleeves and at the neck. [8] German woman *c*. 1130–1150: fitted dress with narrow hip-girdle and long trailing sleeves. [9] French soldier *c*. 1150: metal helmet; chain-mail hood and small cape, tunic and hose. [10] German lady *c*. 1150: fur-lined, orange wool cloak; red gown with blue trimming.

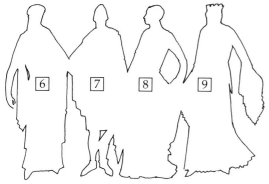

C. 1160–1185

1 Spaniard *c.* 1160: ankle-length cloak with shoulder cape and hood; green undertunic; leather shoes. 2 Italian lady *c.* 1160: gold circlet around braided hair; trailing gown with flared sleeves. 3 French farmworker *c.* 1160: wide-brimmed straw hat; long-sleeved tunic; knee hose; leather boots. 4 Frenchman *c.* 1160–1165: long hair and pointed beard; knee-length tunic with embroidered detail; waist-belt and hip-girdle; undergown decorated with bands of colour; painted leather shoes. 5 Englishman *c.* 1165: cap with yellow band; blue cape fastened at the front with brooch; three-quarter-length overtunic with gold trim.

6 Englishwoman *c.* 1170: long veil; overtunic with waist-belt; long-sleeved undergown; leather shoes. 7 English gentleman *c.* 1185: fur-lined cape; long-sleeved tunic with skirt split at the front; waist-belt with buckle; hose; ankle-boots. 8 Frenchwoman *c.* 1170: turban; V-necked overgown with waist-belt and long trailing sleeves knotted at the ends. 9 French lady *c.* 1185: long hair plaited with ribbons; gown with skirt and flared lower sleeves of finely pleated fabric; double belt and sash.

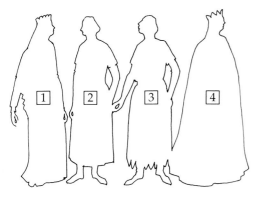

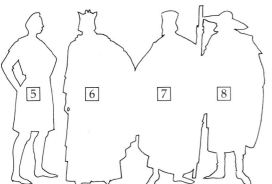

C. 1190–1200

1 English lady *c.* 1190: headdress and veil; wool gown with slight train; waist-belt. 2 German nobleman *c.* 1190–1195: patterned tunic with high collar and wide border at the hem; long hip-belt; ankle-boots. 3 German nobleman *c.* 1190–1195: parti-coloured and parti-patterned tunic with square neckline and dagged hemline; hip-belt; short boots. 4 English queen *c.* 1190: crown and veil; long fur-lined cloak; patterned gown; waist-girdle; embroidered leather gloves.

5 Englishman *c.* 1190: shoulder cape and hood with dagged edges; short tunic with wide embroidered border on hem; hose; leather boots. 6 English king *c.* 1195: jewelled crown; long blue mantle fastened at the front; red tunic; green undergown; red and gold leather shoes. 7 French king *c.* 1200: semi-circular cape held with cord at front; mid-calf-length tunic with bands of embroidery; leather ankle-shoes. 8 Pilgrim *c.* 1200: wide-brimmed straw hat; circular cape with hood; two-tier tunic; footless hose.

C. 1200–1216

1 Peasant woman *c.* 1200: straw hat worn over shoulder cape and hood; linen overgown; leather belt; dark chemise; boots. 2 Monk of Saint Dominic *c.* 1200: cloak and hood; scapular; black boots. 3 Englishman *c.* 1205–1210: long hair and pointed beard; knee-length tunic with embroidered borders; leather ankle-shoes. 4 English lady *c.* 1210: veil and barbette; long cloak; gown with inset bands of embroidery. 5 Dominican nun *c.* 1210: black veil; white barbette; white gown.

6 German soldier *c.* 1200–1215: metal helmet and faceplate; fabric surcoat over chain-mail hood, tunic, hose and mittens; spurs. 7 English knight *c.* 1216: embroidered cloak; tunic with dagged skirt; gauntlets; leather-bound hose. 8 English king *c.* 1215: jewelled crown; long cloak; surcoat; tunic; hose; leather ankle-shoes. 9 English king *c.* 1216: crown; embroidered surcoat; long cloak; patterned hose. 10 English lady *c.* 1216: padded hair dressed under net; sleeveless surcoat; undergown with high neckline and long tight sleeves.

C. 1216–1240

1 Serving woman *c.* 1216–1240: turban worn over white coif; sleeveless surcoat; leather belt; hose with bindings. 2 Italian woman *c.* 1220–1230: head bound with fine linen; tunic with long sleeves and bands of coloured fabric; floor-length undergown. 3 English servant *c.* 1230–1240: short hair; narrow fillet; green and rust parti-coloured tunic with skirt cut into strips; green hose; ankle-boots. 4 Crusader *c.* 1220: complete body suit of chain mail worn under sleeveless surcoat with heraldic decoration; sword belt.

5 English queen *c.* 1230: crown; linen veil and barbette; long fur-lined mantle; leather and gold waist-belt with hanging purse. 6 German noble *c.* 1230–1240: coif over hair; cloak with fur lining; full-length surcoat with long tight sleeves; waist-belt set with metal and stones. 7 Working man *c.* 1230: skull cap and coif; short tunic; drawers; hose; leather ankle-boots. 8 English/German doctor *c.* 1235–1240: small hat with stalk worn over linen bonnet; cowl and hood; long surcoat with hanging sleeves.

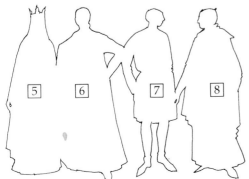

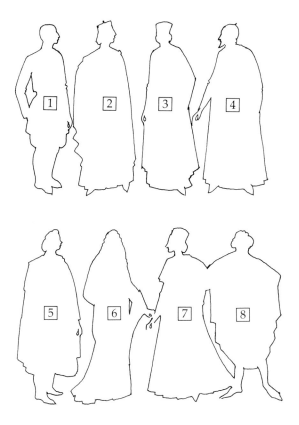

C. 1240–1250

1 Blacksmith *c.* 1240–1250: linen coif; tunic; leather belt with buckle; drawers gathered above the knee; ankle-shoes. 2 French gentleman *c.* 1245: embroidered hat with stalk; patterned cloak; full-length gown with decorative border; purse on waist-belt. 3 Italian lady *c.* 1240–1250: linen headdress over barbette; sleeveless surcoat in embroidered pattern; floor-length undergown with fitted sleeves. 4 Italian tradesman *c.* 1245: stalked cap; long hair and pointed beard; V-necked surcoat split at the front; long-sleeved undertunic.

5 Englishman *c.* 1250: cowl over mid-calf-length coat with wide hanging sleeves; green hose; pointed leather shoes. 6 German girl *c.* 1240–1245: long hair held in place with gold circlet; gown with low square neckline, tight sleeves, trailing cuffs and laced front. 7 German woman *c.* 1245: stiffened linen headdress; linen coif and barbette; hair in snood; wide flowing gown with short sleeves. 8 Frenchman *c.* 1245–1250: curled hair with fringe; gold fillet; cloak; surcoat with long sleeves; waist-belt; patterned hose; leather shoes.

C. 1245–1260

1 German lady *c.* 1245–1250: fabric-covered headdress decorated with precious stones and pearls; barbette and veil; long mantle; gown with V-shaped neckline; waist-belt; embroidered gloves. 2 French soldier *c.* 1245–1250: linen coif; leather tunic with dagged sleeves; chain-mail hose; sword belt. 3 French bishop *c.* 1250–1260: tall embroidered mitre; embroidered cape with braided edges; undergown with embroidered and jewelled hems. 4 Frenchwoman *c.* 1250: headdress and barbette; sleeveless surcoat with open sides; loose undergown with tight sleeves.

5 Italian lady *c.* 1245–1250: surcoat with wide flared sleeves and bands of gold embroidery. 6 German gentleman *c.* 1250: skull cap with stalk; hooded surcoat with open hanging sleeves; boots. 7 English lady *c.* 1255: linen headdress, barbette and veil; sleeveless surcoat; gown with trailing sleeves; embroidered undersleeves. 8 French king *c.* 1255–1260: crown; asymmetric fur-lined cloak with applied goldwork embroidery; floor-length tunic. 9 Frenchman *c.* 1255–1260: short cape and hood with extended point; tunic; waist-belt; hose; ankle-boots.

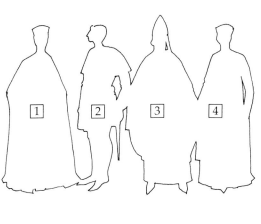

C. 1260–1300

☐ English nobleman *c.* 1260: hat; long hair and beard; full-length coat with fur cape, long hanging sleeves and trailing hem.
☐ Englishman *c.* 1260: hat over coif; three-quarter-length tunic opening at the front; waist-belt; drawers gathered over the knee; patterned hose. ☐ Dutch lady *c.* 1268: veil and gorget; full-length mantle; loose gown; embroidered gloves. ☐ Shepherd *c.* 1260–1275: short cape and hood; tunic with bound hem; long leather boots. ☐ Shepherd *c.* 1260–1275: straw hat over bonnet; shoulder cape and hood; short tunic; leather boots.

☐ French gentleman *c.* 1275: short cloak; tunic with bands of colour; hose; pointed leather shoes. ☐ German nobleman *c.* 1290: sleeveless surcoat with coat of arms at chest level; long tunic.
☐ French lord *c.* 1285–1295: long hair; shoulder cape and hood; gold neck chain; embroidered tunic with tight sleeves and short skirt; waist-belt; hose; long pointed shoes. ☐ French gentleman *c.* 1295–1300: hat with fur trimming; tunic with long tight sleeves and fur-trimmed hem; low waist-belt; hose; pointed shoes.

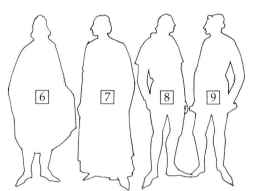

C. 1300–1335

☐ English peasant *c.* 1300–1335: short hair; tunic of coarse fabric; hose attached to short underdrawers; long pointed boots.
☐ English farmworker *c.* 1300–1335: cape and hood with long liripipe; tunic of coarse fabric; hose attached to gathered drawers; short boots with turned-down cuffs. ☐ Englishman *c.* 1300–1325: short hair and beard; cape and hood; tunic buttoning from neck to hem; waist-belt; hose; shoes with long points. ☐ English lady *c.* 1310: barbette and fillet over padded hairnet; full-length mantle; gown with embroidery at neck, wrist and hem, the sleeves buttoned from wrist to elbow; belt and purse.

☐ Young Spanish woman *c.* 1310–1315: twisted fabric fillet; star-embroidered gown with low round neckline, three-quarter-length sleeves and wide cuffs. ☐ English traveller *c.* 1310–1335: hood with short liripipe and short cape with scalloped edges; waist-belt with buckle; hose and garters; long pointed shoes. ☐ Spanish lady *c.* 1325–1330: long hair decorated with narrow fillet of gold flowers; matching earrings and necklace; surcoat with deep armholes; undergown with laced sleeves. ☐ Countrywoman *c.* 1325–1335: short cape and hood over sleeveless surcoat; waist apron.

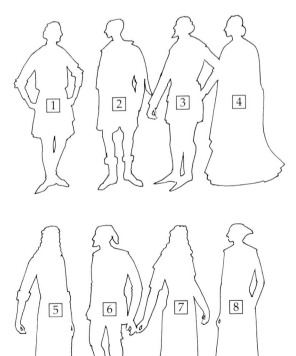

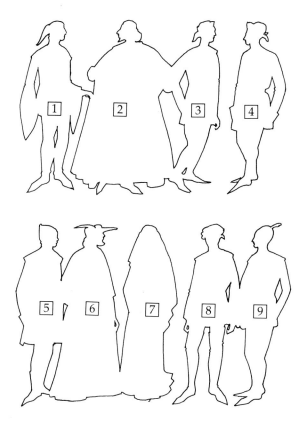

C. 1335–1350

[1] Englishman c. 1335–1340: hood with liripipe and shoulder cape; buttoned cotehardie with long flared sleeves; hip-belt; hose; shoes.
[2] English lord c. 1340: shoulder cape over full-length, fur-lined and -trimmed mantle; gown with buttoned sleeves. [3] Frenchman c. 1335–1340: hat of soft fabric worn over hooded shoulder cape; front-opening tunic of stamped velvet with matching laced sleeves; parti-coloured hose; shoes. [4] English farmer c. 1335–1340: straw hat; coarse tunic with side and front vents; leather mittens; long boots with decorative binding.

[5] Farmworker c. 1340: hood with liripipe wound around the neck; tabard; leather belt; undertunic; boots. [6] Italian merchant c. 1340: peaked felt hat with feather; full-length surcoat with embroidered collar, cuffs and hem, with buttons in sets of three from neck to hem. [7] French lady c. 1340: padded hair under net; long veil; sleeveless surcoat in diagonally striped fabric; undergown with buttoned sleeves. [8] Frenchman c. 1350: liripipe wound around head; scalloped cape; tunic; double belt; thigh-length boots.
[9] Bohemian c. 1350: hat with feather, worn over hooded cape; fitted tunic with padded chest and scalloped hem; soled hose.

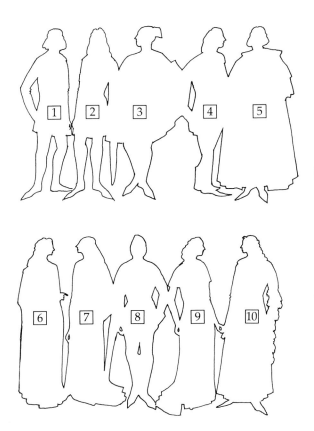

C. 1350–1369

[1] English knight c. 1350: narrow gold fillet; shoulder cape with scalloped edge; parti-coloured padded tunic with decorative buttons and low hip-belt; ankle-boots with long extended points. [2] English lord c. 1350: velvet cape over embroidered surcoat; long tippets on upper sleeves; hip-belt and purse. [3] Traveller c. 1350: cape and hood with liripipe; padded and quilted surcoat with dagged skirt; shoes with long extended points and open fronts. [4] Young Italian c. 1350: parti-coloured and parti-patterned tunic with low neckline; parti-coloured and parti-patterned hose; short, soft leather boots with extended points. [5] Spanish lord c. 1350: deep shoulder cape with hood; long surcoat buttoning from neck to hem; patterned undergown.

[6] Italian lady c. 1355–1360: tabard with button decoration and deep V-shaped neckline; gown with long sleeves. [7] English lady c. 1364: fillet; hair dressed in plaits over ears; veil; parti-coloured gown with square neckline, buttons and long tippets. [8] German knight c. 1369: helmet over chain hood and collar; padded and quilted tunic; hip-belt; gauntlets; leg armour. [9] Spanish girl c. 1365: short-sleeved gown with low square neckline and open sides, buttoned on hip. [10] German lady c. 1369: fillet of twisted fabric; front-buttoning gown with low neckline and dagged tippets; hip-girdle.

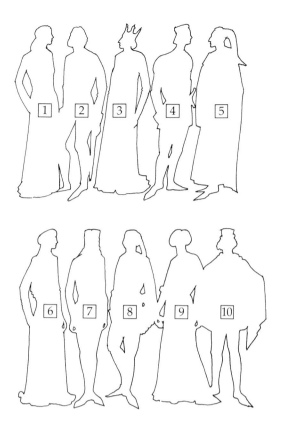

C. 1370–1390

1 Italian lady c. 1370: gown with low square neckline, edged in black, with tight sleeves buttoning to elbow. 2 Spanish soldier c. 1375–1385: tunic with high collar and padded chest over chain armour. 3 French queen c. 1375–1378: tall crown; hair dressed into coiled plaits; surcoat with deep armholes. 4 Italian soldier c. 1380: leather tunic with padded chest and strap fastenings; metal armour on shoulders, arms and legs; gauntlets; spurs. 5 Italian man c. 1385: hood with long liripipe; long sideless surcoat; parti-coloured soled hose.

6 English lady c. 1380: padded roll headdress; long veil; fur-trimmed surcoat. 7 Young German c. 1380–1385: small hat; shoulder cape; padded tunic of embroidered velvet; sash decorated with bells; parti-coloured hose; garter; embroidered shoes. 8 Englishman c. 1385: cape, hood and matching parti-coloured tunic with scalloped and dagged sleeves; soled hose and wooden pattens. 9 Italian lady c. 1380: padded and jewelled roll headdress; fur-trimmed embroidered gown, the skirt with long train; hip-belt. 10 Young German c. 1390: hat with tall crown and padded brim; cape; hooded tunic; belt and purse.

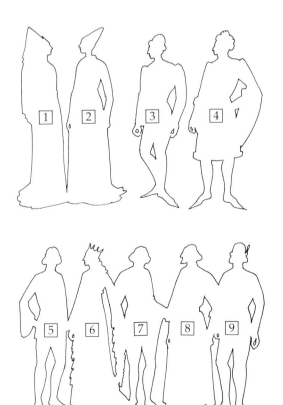

C. 1390–1400

1 Burgundian lady c. 1390: tall headdress with narrow crown and long veil; close-fitting cap; low neckline with solid and transparent infills; wide belt; trailing skirt with bound hem. 2 Burgundian lady c. 1390: tall headdress over cap; gown with low neckline and padded sleeves, trimmed with fur at neck and on trailing hem; high waist-belt. 3 Burgundian gentleman c. 1390: tall hat with padded brim; tunic with high collar and padded chest, hips and sleeves; soled hose. 4 English gentleman c. 1390–1395: padded roll with dagged, draped liripipe crown; fur-trimmed tunic with high collar and full sleeves; waist-belt.

5 Young Frenchman c. 1393: padded surcoat with high collar, bag sleeves and decorative stitching; low hip-belt; long pointed shoes. 6 Spanish lady c. 1395: gown with high waist, low neckline filled with gauze and net, and long dagged sleeves. 7 Young Englishman c. 1396: tunic of stamped velvet, buttoning from high neckline to hem with padded chest and trailing sleeves; striped hose. 8 English scribe c. 1398: surcoat buttoning down the front, with side opening and wide elbow-length sleeves with fur trim. 9 German gentleman c. 1400: hat with tall crown and feather; padded and quilted tunic with dagged skirt; hip-belt.

C. 1400-1415

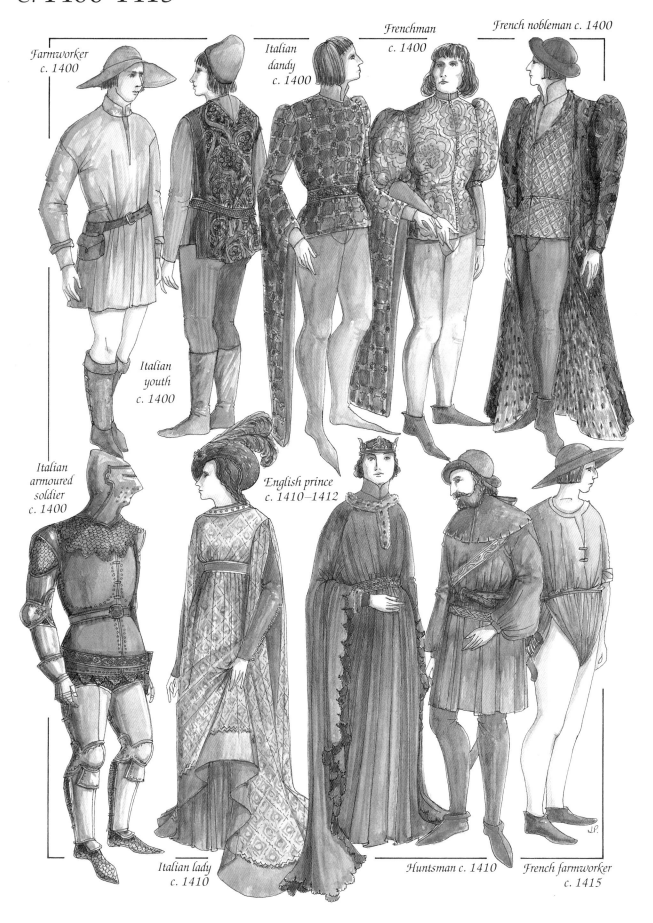

Farmworker
c. 1400

Italian
youth
c. 1400

Italian
dandy
c. 1400

Frenchman
c. 1400

French nobleman c. 1400

Italian
armoured
soldier
c. 1400

English prince
c. 1410–1412

Italian lady
c. 1410

Huntsman c. 1410

French farmworker
c. 1415

C. 1415-1426

English queen
c. 1415

French lord
c. 1415

Englishman
c. 1420–1425

German woman
c. 1425

French farmer
c. 1425

French butcher c. 1425

French housekeeper c. 1425

Chambermaid c. 1426

C. 1430

English lord

Frenchwoman

Frenchman

Burgundian man

German lady

English falconer

English lady

English gentleman

French nobleman

English lady

59

c. 1433-1435

German man
c. 1433

English legal man
c. 1435

English lady
c. 1435

German lady
c. 1435

German man
c. 1435

French lady c. 1435

Dutch lady c. 1435

Dutch nobleman c. 1435

c. 1435-1440

Frenchwoman

English nursemaid

German gentleman

English milkmaid

French lady

English scribe

Burgundian man

German gentleman

English youth

English gentleman

C. 1440

Dutch
nobleman

Burgundian
dandy

Burgundian lady

French dandy

French lady

French gentleman

Dutch lady

Flemish lady

62

c. 1440-1450

Frenchwoman c. 1445

French peasant woman c. 1445

French lady c. 1445

English gentleman c. 1440–1445

Flemish workman c. 1445

French lady c. 1445

German youth c. 1445–1450

Burgundian gentleman c. 1445–1450

French peasant woman c. 1445

French servant c. 1445–1450

c. 1450

Italian noblewoman

English lady

Italian workman

Italian lady

Italian servant

German youth

French workman

English lord

French noblewoman

German youth

64

c. 1450

German soldier

Italian servant

Italian girl

Spanish workman

Italian merchant

Italian woman

French youth

French farmworker

Dutchwoman
c. 1450

Frenchwoman
c. 1450

Flemish woman
c. 1450

German
woman
c. 1452

English serving
woman c. 1455

English morris dancer
c. 1450–1455

English morris dancer
c. 1450–1455

French farmer c. 1455

c. 1455-1470

Italian youth
c. 1455

Venetian prince
c. 1455

Italian man
c. 1457

Dutchwoman
c. 1465

French
armoured
soldier
c. 1461

German youth
c. 1470

German
girl
c. 1470

Italian youth
c. 1470

German lady c. 1470

C. 1470-1475

Italian gentleman c. 1470

German lady c. 1470

Spanish lady c. 1470

Young Italian woman c. 1470

Flemish youth c. 1475

French youth c. 1475

English gentleman c. 1475

French gentleman c. 1475

C. 1475-1485

Italian archer
c. 1475

Frenchwoman
c. 1475

Flemish musician
c. 1475

Venetian dandy
c. 1485

French girl
c. 1475–1480

French nobleman
c. 1485

Spanish noblewoman
c. 1475

French court lady c. 1485

C. 1490

Italian gentleman

Italian lady

Italian woman

Young Italian man

Italian girl

Italian girl

Italian merchant

Italian dandy

c. 1490-1500

Flemish lady
c. 1490

Italian gentleman
c. 1495

French lady
c. 1496

French
huntsman
c. 1498

French youth
c. 1498

English lady
c. 1498

English lady c. 1498

English nobleman
c. 1499–1500

Frenchman c. 1490–1495

French lady c. 1495

Florentine lady c. 1495

French gentleman c. 1495

Venetian lady c. 1498

English dandy c. 1498

Venetian lady c. 1498

Italian noblewoman c. 1498

French gentleman c. 1500

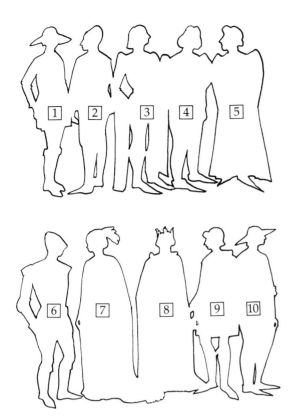

C. 1400-1415

[1] Farmworker *c.* 1400: hat with wide brim; undertunic with collar; mid-calf-length overtunic; leather belt and pouch; gaiters with side fastenings. [2] Italian youth *c.* 1400: brimless felt hat; embroidered tabard; parti-coloured hose; knee-length boots. [3] Italian dandy *c.* 1400: embroidered tunic with high collar, tight bodice and long trailing sleeves; parti-coloured soled hose with extended points. [4] Frenchman *c.* 1400: short tunic buttoned from neck to hem with straw-filled top sleeves; joined hose; short leather ankle-shoes. [5] French nobleman *c.* 1400: hat with draped crown and padded brim; embroidered and fur-trimmed tunic; fur-lined floor-length coat with large sleeves; short leather ankle-shoes.

[6] Italian armoured soldier *c.* 1400: leather, metal and chain armour. [7] Italian lady *c.* 1410: fur hat with feather and brooch trim; long hair; overgown of patterned silk with high waistline and long trailing sleeves; undergown with buttoned sleeves. [8] English prince *c.* 1410–1412: gold crown set with precious stones; velvet robe with long, trailing, dagged sleeves. [9] Huntsman *c.* 1410: hat; cape and hood; knee-length tunic; sword belt; hose; short boots. [10] French farmworker *c.* 1415: wide-brimmed straw hat; short shift tucked into waist-belt; ankle-boots.

C. 1415-1426

[1] English queen *c.* 1415: gold crown; hair dressed around ears; necklace with pendant; fur-trimmed overgown with wide neckline, the armholes cut down to hip level; tight-fitting undergown. [2] French lord *c.* 1415: hat with padded roll headdress and drapery; parti-coloured dagged robe with long, trailing, dagged sleeves; waist-belt; soled hose with long points. [3] Englishman *c.* 1420–1425: fur-lined and -trimmed coat; short undertunic with button opening and bag sleeves; joined hose with leather soles. [4] German woman *c.* 1425: pleated bonnet worn over tight-fitting hood and cape; long fur-trimmed mantle; gown with laced opening.

[5] French butcher *c.* 1425: turban; short close-fitting tunic with button opening; long apron; boots. [6] French farmer *c.* 1425: small hat; short tunic; leather waist-belt with tool holder; rolled-down hose; boots. [7] French housekeeper *c.* 1425: cotton veil with scalloped edge; simple gown with elbow-length sleeves and mid-calf-length skirt; apron; soled hose. [8] Chambermaid *c.* 1426: short dark veil; simple gown with high waistline; long apron from under bust.

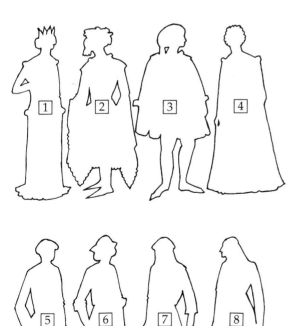

C. 1430

1 English lord: short cropped hair; black velvet collar; fur-trimmed tunic of yellow and black patterned brocade; white soled hose.
2 Frenchwoman: black veil; orange wrap-around gown with fur cuffs; black undergown; large white apron; bag hanging from waist-belt. 3 Frenchman: red hat cut in sections; white chemise; red undertunic; grey wool tunic; large white apron; leather shoes with straps. 4 Burgundian man: tall hat topped with feather; full-length gown with high collar and large puffed sleeves; blue hose with long points. 5 German lady: hair decorated with wreath of fabric leaves; gown with high waistline and long trailing sleeves with daggings.

6 English falconer: fur hat; orange undergown; leather tunic with blanket-stitch edges; red hose; short boots. 7 English lady: heart-shaped headdress of tiny fabric petals; richly patterned gown with wide fur-lined sleeves and embroidered borders. 8 English gentleman: padded roll headdress with dagged drapery; long hair; tunic of richly patterned and embroidered fabric with velvet trimming; hose; embroidered shoes. 9 French nobleman: padded roll headdress with dagged drapery; long, green silk gown with gold embroidery and long trailing sleeves; red leather belt and purse.
10 English lady: heart-shaped padded roll headdress over gold mesh cap; veil tied under the chin; bright-blue gown in star pattern with long, trailing, embroidered sleeves.

C. 1433–1435

1 German man c. 1433: long cloak with side button fastening; knee-length tunic; leather belt and bag; wool hose; leather shoes.
2 English legal man c. 1435: fur hat bound with silk, worn over the shoulder; ankle-length tunic; leather belt with bag and pen holder; soled hose. 3 English lady c. 1435: red and gold jewelled headdress in the form of horns; long transparent veil and matching collar; long gown with open trailing sleeves; undergown with large bag sleeves. 4 German lady c. 1435: braided hair dressed over the ears; gown with fur trimming and trailing fur sleeves.

5 French lady c. 1435: padded roll headdress with transparent veil; red velvet gown with large bag sleeves; pleated undergown.
6 Dutch lady c. 1435: padded roll headdress decorated with dagged material and brooch; floor-length mantle with bound edges; gown with high-waist detail and bag sleeves. 7 Dutch nobleman c. 1435: hat with draped, dagged fabric; gold neck chain and pendant; high-necked tunic; wide sleeves with dagged decoration; low hip-belt.
8 German man c. 1435: wide-brimmed hat over hood and cape with dagged edges; tunic with front-laced opening; low hip-belt; soled hose.

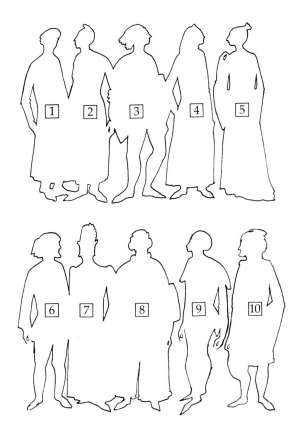

C. 1435–1440

[1] Frenchwoman: white linen turban; white chemise with drawstring neck; blue dress; white apron; black soled hose.
[2] English nursemaid: red cap; hair dressed into nets; deep white linen collar; ankle-length dress; hip-belt and bag. [3] German gentleman: draped hat with falling dagged edges; tunic with front-laced opening and wide turned-back sleeves with dagged edges; hip-belt; white hose. [4] English milkmaid: linen headdress and veil; dress with low scooped neckline and side-lacing; white linen apron and underskirt; boots. [5] French lady: white linen bonnet with topknot, tied under the chin; white linen collar with scalloped edges; long gown with flared sleeves; high waist-sash.

[6] English scribe: hat with padded brim; tunic with laced opening; leather belt and pouch; black hose; leather shoes. [7] Burgundian man: tall hat with narrow brim and feather trim; full-length gown; waist-belt; shoes with long points. [8] German gentleman: fur hat; short hair and beard; knee-length embroidered undergown; full-length coat with fur lining and trim; waist-belt; long boots.
[9] English youth: dark-green padded roll headdress; tunic with dagged detail on the short sleeves and the skirt; parti-coloured hose and boots. [10] English gentleman: draped and padded hat; short pointed beard; patterned tunic with flared sleeves; striped hose; shoes with button trim.

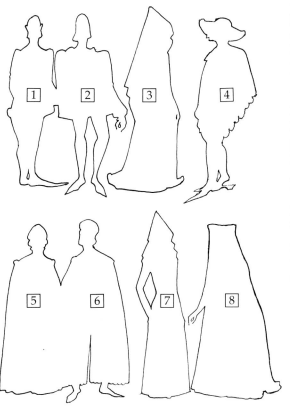

C. 1440

[1] Dutch nobleman: green hat with tall crown and narrow red brim; green tunic slashed at the elbows and trimmed with fur; red undertunic; grey hose; rust-coloured leather shoes with points.
[2] Burgundian dandy: tall, brimless, black hat with brooch trim; short red and gold brocade tunic trimmed with fur; black soled hose. [3] Burgundian lady: tall, pointed headdress with fine transparent veil; fur- and braid-trimmed gown with belt under the bust. [4] French dandy: felt hat with wide brim and narrow fur trimming; cape and cloak with scalloped and dagged edges; short pleated tunic with leather belt and pouch; cream soled hose; wooden pattens.

[5] French lady: padded roll headdress with brooch trim; gown with high fur-trimmed collar and open fur-lined sleeves trailing to the ground; high waist-belt. [6] French gentleman: blue draped hat; fur-trimmed tunic with high standing collar and pleated bodice and skirt; decorative neck collar of tiny bells; grey soled hose. [7] Dutch lady: tall black headdress with fine transparent veil; gown of black brocade with long tight sleeves, the neckline square with transparent infill. [8] Flemish lady: jewelled and embroidered headdress; veil with scalloped edge; high-waisted gown with long, open, trailing sleeves; long, tight, embroidered sleeves.

C. 1440–1450

1 English gentleman c. 1440–1445: large hat with wide brim; cape and hood; tunic with dagged and scalloped decoration and open, fur-trimmed bag sleeves; hose; ankle-shoes. 2 Frenchwoman c. 1445: large padded roll headdress; gown with tight bodice and front-laced opening, the skirt looped up into belt; wool underskirt. 3 French peasant woman c. 1445: white linen bonnet; ankle-length dress with wide transparent collar; large apron. 4 French lady c. 1445: tall headdress with gauze veil; embroidered gown with transparent collar and cuffs. 5 French lady c. 1445: red headdress with long back veil; gold and black embroidered gown with long, trailing, open sleeves.

6 Flemish workman c. 1445: small cap; red tunic; leather belt; footless hose; black leather ankle-shoes. 7 French peasant woman c. 1445: white linen turban; striped linen dress; short-sleeved overbodice; petticoat; hose; ankle-shoes. 8 French servant c. 1445–1450: red cap with topknot, worn over white linen bonnet; grey dress with wide lower sleeves; large black apron. 9 Burgundian gentleman c. 1445–1450: fur-trimmed hat with feather; brocade coat with fur-trimmed open sleeves; soled hose. 10 German youth c. 1445–1450: fabric hat trimmed with feather; fine linen shirt with embroidered decoration; tunic with slashed sleeves; leather belt; dagger; joined hose.

C. 1450

1 Italian noblewoman: padded roll headdress; long robe with high collar and long, trailing, open sleeves; high waist-belt. 2 English lady: turban of fabric leaves with brooch decoration; gown with long open sleeves cut into leaf shapes; high waist-belt. 3 Italian workman: linen cap; thick wool jacket; pleated tunic; knee-length hose; short boots. 4 Italian servant: dark-blue undertunic; skirt of overrobe tucked into leather belt; footless knee-length hose. 5 Italian lady: small gold tiara; hair dressed over the ears; gown with trailing skirt and flared sleeves in bright-blue cloth decorated with silver stars; low hip-belt.

6 French workman: close-fitting cap; white undershirt; jerkin with short sleeves and laced fastening; joined hose; ankle-boots. 7 English lord: fur hat; knee-length robe with fur trim; low belt; ankle-shoes. 8 German youth: narrow fillet; shirt with padded collar and full sleeves; tunic with low neckline and long tight sleeves with slashed detail; parti-coloured and parti-patterned hose; shoes with long points. 9 French noblewoman: tall horned headdress with draped veil; hair dressed into coils over the ears; gown with long tight sleeves, fur cuffs, collar and hem. 10 German youth: draped fabric turban; hip-length coat with short sleeves and braided decoration; pleated shirt with embroidered trim; joined hose; ankle-boots.

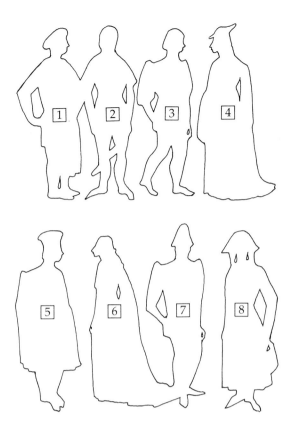

C. 1450

1 Spanish workman: padded roll headdress with long fringed ends; buttoned shirt; wrapover tunic; apron threaded over leather belt; ankle-shoes. 2 German soldier: metal helmet over chain hood and cape; padded leather tunic; double leather sword belt; footless hose worn over ankle-boots. 3 Italian servant: dark undertunic with high standing collar and tight sleeves; short orange velvet tunic with large sleeves and short pleated skirt; parti-coloured joined hose; knee-length boots. 4 Italian girl: small three-cornered hat; long curled hair; gold necklace set with stones; long gown with large linen collar and flared sleeves; high waist-belt.

5 Italian merchant: felt hat worn over skull cap; dark-green coat with open bag sleeves; dark-grey underrobe buttoned from neck to hem; waist-sash; soled hose. 6 Italian woman: pink velvet gown with high waist and hanging bag sleeves; purple silk undergown with long, tight, buttoned sleeves. 7 French youth: tall felt hat with narrow brim; stitched and pleated tunic with full sleeves with decorative slashes; dagger suspended from leather belt; blue hose; embroidered shoes. 8 French farmworker: black headdress and veil; blue dress with skirt caught into waist-sash; quilted petticoat.

C. 1450–1455

1 Dutchwoman c. 1450: turban covering hair and ears; high-waisted sleeveless smock; red wool undergown with bag sleeves; petticoat; dark hose; leather mules. 2 Frenchwoman c. 1450: red headdress with white turned-back brim and long point at the back; wool gown with boat-shaped neckline, full skirt, fur-trimmed cuffs and hem; wide belt. 3 Flemish woman c. 1450: bonnet with long point and frilled skirt; wool dress with deep peplum overfold; self-fabric belt; blue undergown; leather mules. 4 German woman c. 1452: linen turban; dress with square neckline, high waist and gathered skirt; thick wool chemise; leather mules.

5 English morris dancer c. 1450–1455: tall hat with upturned brim and long scarf; parti-coloured tunic, skirt and hose decorated with bells; short boots. 6 English morris dancer c. 1450–1455: tall hat and hose decorated with bells; tunic with wide sleeves and short pleated skirt; ankle-shoes with narrow cuff. 7 English serving woman c. 1455: linen veil held with draped circlet; robe with low round neckline infilled with linen scarf, peplum and full skirt; belt; soled hose. 8 French farmer c. 1455: hat bound with scarf; short jerkin with threaded leather fastening; short cotton trunks; leather ankle-boots.

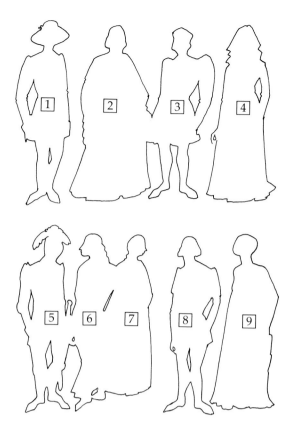

C. 1455–1470

1 Italian youth c. 1455: white hat with wide brim trimmed with red feather; red velvet coat with button fastening, the chest and full sleeves padded with straw; laced boots. 2 Venetian prince c. 1455: cap and undergown of red silk; gold and green re-embroidered brocade robe with wide scalloped sleeves. 3 Italian man c. 1457: velvet cap; fur-trimmed robe of stamped velvet with padded chest and sleeves; soled hose. 4 Dutchwoman c. 1465: tall headdress with fine transparent veil; low-necked gown with black collar, infill and belt, pleated skirt, long tight sleeves and white cuffs.

5 French armoured soldier c. 1461: metal helmet with visor and feather decoration; jointed metal armour worn over suit of chain mail; sword belt. 6 German youth c. 1470: long flowing hair; narrow, twisted gold fillet; tunic sewn in sections of different coloured fabric; parti-coloured and parti-patterned joined hose. 7 German girl c. 1470: jewelled circlet around unbound hair; necklace of gold and pearls; simple gown with braided edges; pleated underrobe. 8 Italian youth c. 1470: short tunic with small standing collar and short sleeves; waist-sash; undersleeves embroidered with silver stars; hose; knee-length boots. 9 German lady c. 1470: large padded roll headdress; loose-fitting gown with wide neckline and bound edges; blue underrobe.

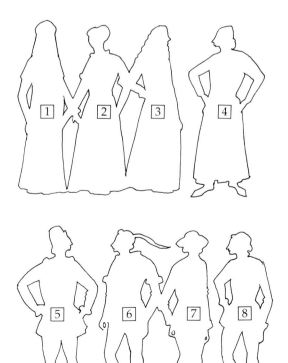

C. 1470–1475

1 German lady c. 1470: padded roll headdress with brooch trim and long transparent veil; loose-fitting gown with low square neckline; richly embroidered undersleeves. 2 Spanish lady c. 1470: headdress with padded brim embroidered with gold thread and worn over gold net cap; gown with V-shaped neckline trimmed with fur to match short sleeves and split skirt. 3 Young Italian woman c. 1470: long curled hair; circlet of ceramic flowers and leaves; high-waisted gown with low V-shaped neckline, infilled with red silk and edged with gold braid. 4 Italian gentleman c. 1470: small red skull cap; black undertunic with high standing collar; full-length coat of re-embroidered gold silk brocade with lilac satin collar; narrow waist-belt and pouch.

5 French youth c. 1475: soft felt hat with brooch trim; green velvet tunic with rich brown fur trim; hose; black ankle-boots. 6 Flemish youth c. 1475: fabric hat with long feather trim; fur-trimmed brocade tunic, the skirt with flat pleats; black undertunic. 7 English gentleman c. 1475: green velvet hat with deep fur brim; tunic with matching fur trim; hose; ankle-shoes. 8 French gentleman c. 1475: velvet hat with fur brim; brocade tunic with low square neckline and pleated skirt; black hose; red leather ankle-shoes.

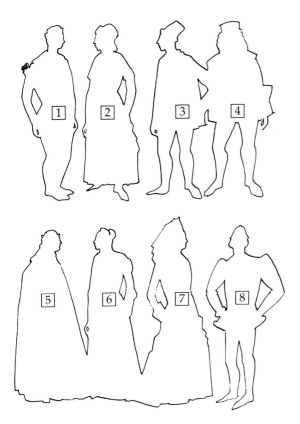

C. 1475–1485

[1] Italian archer *c.* 1475: leather hat; wool undertunic and hood; leather tunic with top-stitching; waist-belt; joined hose and codpiece; ankle-shoes. [2] Frenchwoman *c.* 1475: white linen cap with upturned brim; dress with bound square neckline and short sleeves, the brocade skirt caught into narrow waist-belt; full petticoat. [3] Flemish musician *c.* 1475: matching parti-coloured outfit of tall hat with padded brim, tabard and sewn hose. [4] Venetian dandy *c.* 1485: small hat; long curled hair; pleated shirt with full sleeves; very short coat with fur collar and cuffs; leather gauntlets with gold embroidery; parti-coloured hose and codpiece.

[5] French girl *c.* 1475–1480: long flowing hair; wreath of leaves; long velvet mantle over brocade dress with tight bodice and sleeves. [6] Spanish noblewoman *c.* 1475: narrow tiara; hair dressed away from the face; dress with fitted bodice, tight sleeves with slashes and skirt worn over frame of wire hoops. [7] French court lady *c.* 1485: tall jewelled headdress with fine veil; long, trailing, brocade gown with fur trimming; embroidered belt worn under the bust. [8] French nobleman *c.* 1485: small hat; brocade tunic with padded, stitched bodice and fur-trimmed skirt; large padded sleeves; hose; ankle-shoes.

C. 1490

[1] Italian gentleman: small black hat; long curled hair; pink underrobe with tight sleeves; coat with open bag sleeves lined to match green silk collar; hose; leather mules. [2] Italian lady: small cap edged with pearls; brocade gown with tightly fitted open bodice and skirt to show the undergown; skirts worn over wire hoop. [3] Italian woman: long hair held by wide embroidered kerchief; loose-fitting overgown with deep V-shaped neckline and fur cuffs; undergown with laced bodice and pleated skirt. [4] Young Italian man: small black hat with brooch trim; short coat with fur collar and cuffs; gold neck chain; parti-coloured hose; leather shoes.

[5] Italian girl: linen cap tied under the chin; transparent chemise; fine linen undergown pulled through slashes in the sleeves of patterned brocade gown. [6] Italian girl: mesh cap; gold and bead necklace; high-waisted velvet dress with patterned velvet sleeves and underbodice. [7] Italian merchant: small hat; long hair and short beard; mid-calf-length coat; painted leather belt and hip bag. [8] Italian dandy: small red cap with feather decoration; short jerkin with slashed sleeves and side seams; parti-coloured joined hose and codpiece.

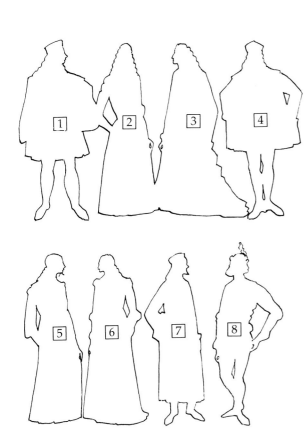

C. 1490–1500

[1] Flemish lady c. 1490: headdress with wide turned-back brim; gown with fitted bodice and low square neckline with transparent infill; hip-girdle with inset stones and long tassels. [2] Italian gentleman c. 1495: velvet hat with padded brim; gold neck chain; tunic with pleated skirt and flared sleeves; striped hose; leather ankle-boots. [3] French lady c. 1496: black veil; gown of embroidered brocade with V-shaped neckline and wide flared sleeves; hip-girdle. [4] French huntsman c. 1498: hat with wide brim and feather trim; tunic with side button fastening and short pleated skirt; joined hose with contrasting colour inset pattern; ankle-boots.

[5] French youth c. 1498: small hat; short tunic decorated with slashes and embroidery; joined hose; nether hose and codpiece; flat shoes with round toes. [6] English lady c. 1498: headdress and veil over small cap; low square neckline with embroidered edges to match flared sleeve hem and waist-belt. [7] English lady c. 1498: linen headdress, cap and veil; velvet gown with wide fur cuffs and matching fur-trimmed hem. [8] English nobleman c. 1499–1500: small fabric hat with upturned brim; short coat with large collar and cuffs of fox fur; embroidered tunic; joined hose and codpiece; flat shoes with blunt toes.

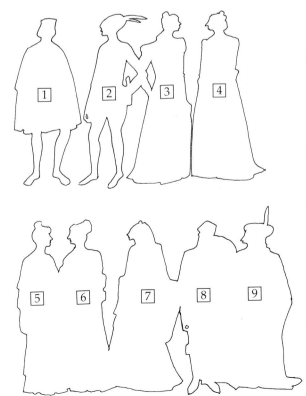

C. 1490–1500

[1] French gentleman c. 1495: small fabric hat; coat with open hanging sleeves and large fur trim; brocade tunic with slashed bodice and sleeves; joined hose; codpiece; round-toed leather shoes with slashed decoration. [2] Frenchman c. 1490–1495: hat with two feathers worn over small cap; green tunic with button fastening; sleeves in contrasting colour; hose with inset pattern; slashed shoes. [3] French lady c. 1495: gown with low neckline infilled with silk scarf, tight bodice with decorative tuck held by brooch, and short draped oversleeves. [4] Florentine lady c. 1495: hair dressed over the ears and into back bun; drop earrings and matching necklace; quilted and jewelled undergown; tabard of stamped and embroidered velvet.

[5] Venetian lady c. 1498: natural and false hair dressed on top of the head; necklace; gown with low neckline, tiny bodice with braided edge and slashed sleeves tied with small cords. [6] Venetian lady c. 1498: pearl necklace; low-necked gown with short, black velvet bodice and embroidered sleeves tied with small cords. [7] Italian noblewoman c. 1498: padded, embroidered and beaded fabric tiara with black velvet veil; gown with tight bodice, low square neckline and large cuffs, the skirt worn over frame. [8] English dandy c. 1498: small and large hat with feathers, worn over one shoulder; pleated shirt; waist-tunic with large padded and slashed sleeves; patterned hose. [9] French gentleman c. 1500: fur hat decorated with ribbons and feathers; long brocade coat with fur collar and open bag sleeves.

c. 1500-1505

German housekeeper c. 1500

German huntsman c. 1500

German huntsman c. 1500

Flemish workman c. 1504

Flemish workman c. 1504

German lady c. 1500

Italian lady c. 1505

German lady c. 1500–1505

Flemish countrywoman c. 1505

Flemish farmworker
c. 1505

German lady
c. 1506

German
noblewoman
c. 1510

Flemish
farmworker
c. 1505

German nobleman
c. 1514

German lady
c. 1515

German merchant c. 1510

German lady c. 1514

c. 1515-1525

German scholar
c. 1515–1520

German woman
c. 1520

German lady
c. 1520

German gentleman
c. 1520

German gentleman
c. 1525

Flemish peasant
c. 1525

Flemish countryman c. 1525

Flemish countrywoman c. 1525

German soldier
c. 1530

French peasant
c. 1535

German man c. 1534

Spanish king
c. 1530

English lord
c. 1535

German woman
c. 1535

Spanish queen c. 1535

English lady c. 1535

C. 1536-1541

English queen
c. 1536

English princess
c. 1541

German man
c. 1540

Spanish
gentleman
c. 1541

Venetian official
c. 1540

English lord
c. 1540

German gentleman c. 1540

French lady c. 1541

c. 1541-1550

English king
c. 1541

English queen
c. 1545

English prince
c. 1547

Viennese
archduke
c. 1541

Spanish king
c. 1550

French gentleman c. 1550   Italian official c. 1550   Italian lady c. 1550

c. 1550

Italian lady

French king

Italian princess

Italian gentleman

Italian servant

English housemaid

Belgian peasant

Italian lady

C. 1551-1555

German gentleman
c. 1551

German princess
c. 1551

Portuguese queen
c. 1552

English queen
c. 1554

French lady
c. 1555

Spanish prince
c. 1555

Italian lady c. 1555

Spanish gentleman c. 1555

c. 1557-1560

Italian lady
c. 1558

French gentleman
c. 1558

Italian gentleman
c. 1558

French nobleman
c. 1557

German woman
c. 1558

Italian lady
c. 1560

Italian lady
c. 1560

Spanish general c. 1560

C. 1560

Spanish gentleman

German councillor

Italian youth

Spanish soldier

German lady

Swedish king

Englishwoman

German man

c. 1560-1565

Spanish man
c. 1560

English groom
c. 1560

German baker
c. 1560

German man
c. 1560

Spanish lady
c. 1565

Italian man
c. 1565

Belgian countryman c. 1560

Italian gentlewoman c. 1565

C. 1565-1575

French gentleman
c. 1565

Flemish
peasant
c. 1565

English worker
c. 1565

French milkmaid
c. 1565

German
gentleman
c. 1570

English lady
c. 1575

English statesman c. 1575   English butler c. 1575

English queen c. 1575

c. 1580

Spanish princess

Italian man

German gentleman

Spanish lady

Italian gentleman

Italian lady

French gentleman

French gentleman

c. 1580-1590

French countess
c. 1580

English royal
guard c. 1580

English lady
c. 1583

Spanish princess
c. 1584

German
courtier
c. 1585

Dutchwoman
c. 1587

Spanish princess c. 1585

Spanish gentleman c. 1588

English lord
c. 1590

c. 1590-1595

German man
c. 1590

Swedish princess
c. 1590

Italian man
c. 1590

German gentleman
c. 1590

French servant
c. 1590

English queen
c. 1592

Italian lady c. 1590

Venetian gentleman c. 1595

c. 1595-1600

Spanish lady
c. 1595

Spanish princess
c. 1595

German gentleman
c. 1595–1598

English soldier
c. 1595–1597

Englishman
c. 1598

English lady
c. 1600

English countrywoman c. 1600

English statesman c. 1600

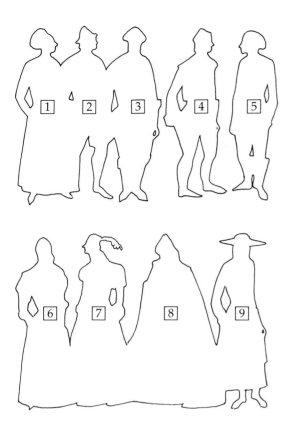

C. 1500–1505

1 German housekeeper *c.* 1500: white linen cap, collar, shoulder cape and apron; ankle-length dress with tight sleeves and bodice; leather belt and purse. 2 German huntsman *c.* 1500: hat with narrow brim; jacket with wide slashed sleeves; long, leather, footless boots worn over ankle-shoes. 3 German huntsman *c.* 1500: small fabric hat; short jacket; narrow leather belt; striped hose and codpiece; knee-length boots. 4 Flemish workman *c.* 1504: leather hat; shoulder cape; neck scarf; tunic with waist-sash; hose; long boots open at back. 5 Flemish workman *c.* 1504: combined cape and hood; tunic with tie belt; wool hose; slashed leather boots with scalloped cuff.

6 German lady *c.* 1500: hair parted in middle and decorated with circlet of beads; necklace and matching earrings; gown with slashed sleeves and bodice; skirt braided and banded with embroidery, mounted over frame. 7 German lady *c.* 1500–1505: tiny gold mesh cap decorated with long ostrich feather; pearl necklace with pendant; wide scooped neckline with embroidered edge; puffed sleeves with slashes. 8 Italian lady *c.* 1505: hair dressed into gold net; gown with tight bodice and full skirt worn under patterned velvet travelling cape. 9 Flemish countrywoman *c.* 1505: wide-brimmed straw hat; linen scarf; laced bodice; skirt tucked into waist-belt; linen underskirt; leather mules.

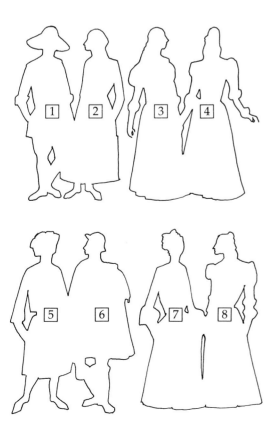

C. 1505–1515

1 Flemish farmworker *c.* 1505: straw hat with wide brim; cape and hood; T-shaped tunic; leather belt and bag; hose of coarse material; shoes with strap. 2 Flemish farmworker *c.* 1505: stiff white veil; wrap-around dress; skirt tucked into leather waist-belt; wool underskirt; shoes with strap. 3 German lady *c.* 1506: pearl earrings and necklace; shoulder cape; gown with tight-laced bodice; puffed and slashed sleeves. 4 German noblewoman *c.* 1510: fine gold mesh cap; transparent collar with wired edge; puffed, slashed and embroidered sleeves; skirt worn over frame.

5 German merchant *c.* 1510: hat with wide, upturned, scalloped brim; tunic of stamped velvet with braid trim; hose; shoes with strap. 6 German nobleman *c.* 1514: fur-trimmed hat; knee-length coat, tunic and hose decorated with tiny slashes; tied fringed garters; flat leather shoes. 7 German lady *c.* 1514: gold embroidered turban; white feather and brooch trim; gown of gold brocade and red velvet. 8 German lady *c.* 1515: gold jewellery set with stones; brown silk gown with pink sleeves embroidered with gold thread.

C. 1515–1525

1 German scholar *c.* 1515–1520: small hat with stalk; gown with open hanging sleeves; wide yoke at the front and back, with deep cartridge pleats; ankle-shoes. 2 German woman *c.* 1520: padded turban; linen veil; small shoulder cape; top half of bodice and sleeves of finely spotted silk; skirt and lower bodice of blue velvet trimmed with red silk. 3 German lady *c.* 1520: hair enclosed under fine mesh net bonnet; drop earrings; high jewelled collar; low round neckline covered with fine linen; puffed and slashed sleeves; skirt with large bands around hem, worn over frame. 4 German gentleman *c.* 1520: small hat with stalk; floor-length coat with fur lining and trim; long hanging sleeves.

5 Flemish countryman *c.* 1525: cap with upturned brim at back; small cape and hood with scalloped edges; T-shaped tunic with bound hem; hose; leather gaiters. 6 German gentleman *c.* 1525: leather hat with scalloped and upturned brim; fur-lined and fur-trimmed sleeveless coat; flat shoes with instep strap. 7 Flemish countrywoman *c.* 1525: straw hat with threaded band, worn over green wool hood; tunic dress worn over black petticoat; large linen tabard. 8 Flemish peasant *c.* 1525: white linen veil; dark shoulder scarf worn over linen bodice; sash; waist apron; skirt with bound hem; leather mules.

C. 1530–1535

1 Spanish king *c.* 1530: black velvet hat with feather trim; doublet with large banded and tiered puffed sleeves; embroidered undertunic; fur-lined and -trimmed overcoat; slashed breeches and codpiece. 2 German soldier *c.* 1530: wide cap trimmed with feathers; tunic, codpiece and knee-breeches decorated with tiny slashes. 3 French peasant *c.* 1535: straw hat with wide brim; short tunic; footless, joined hose with codpiece. 4 German man *c.* 1534: fabric cap with stiffened brim; narrow neck and wrist ruffs; long doublet trimmed with gold braid; fur-lined and -trimmed short overcoat with puffed upper sleeves; padded and slashed breeches; silk garters tied at the knee; slashed shoes.

5 Spanish queen *c.* 1535: elaborately plaited hair; pearl earrings and necklace; gown with low square neckline; wide trailing sleeves slit and pinned with brooches at the front; tight bodice; full split skirt worn over brocade underskirt and wire support frame. 6 English lord *c.* 1535: velvet cap; trimmed moustache and beard; short coat with large fur collar to hem; full padded and fur-trimmed sleeves; leather gloves. 7 German woman *c.* 1535: plaited hair held with braid at ears and decorated with pearls; velvet gown with low square neckline; tight bodice; sleeves with large turned-back cuffs; embroidered skirt worn over frame. 8 English lady *c.* 1535: stiff, kennel-shaped headdress of black cloth worn over close-fitting, padded turban; gown with very large turned-back fur cuffs; jewelled waist-girdle with suspended purse.

C. 1536–1541

1 English queen *c.* 1536: kennel-shaped headdress with shoulder-length black veil; jewelled necklace, pendant, brooches and pins; gown with very large turned-back cuffs covered with gold mesh; padded false undersleeves. 2 English princess *c.* 1541: brocade dress with wide square-cut neckline; split skirt over re-embroidered underskirt; jewelled waist-belt and pendant. 3 German man *c.* 1540: fabric hat gathered on to narrow stiffened brim; wrapover tunic with scalloped collar; breeches; garters with decorative slashes. 4 Spanish gentleman *c.* 1541: embroidered hat trimmed with feathers; short coat with fur collar; doublet, breeches and codpiece of matching slashed decoration; leather gloves and shoes.

5 Venetian official *c.* 1540: small hat; ankle-length coat with full bag sleeves; short undertunic; joined hose; leather mules and gloves. 6 German gentleman *c.* 1540: large hat decorated with ruched ribbons, feathers and brooches; wide neck ruff; doublet and breeches trimmed with gold braid; velvet coat with large puffed sleeves, lined in red silk. 7 English lord *c.* 1540: flat silk hat trimmed with brooch and feathers; doublet decorated with gold embroidery and braid; short red silk coat; padded breeches; leather shoes with decorative slashes. 8 French lady *c.* 1541: black velvet veil embroidered with gold threads; grey velvet dress with fine gold embroidery around neck and down bodice and skirt; wide sleeves with black cuffs; waist-girdle and pendant.

C. 1541–1550

1 Viennese archduke *c.* 1541: velvet hat trimmed with feathers; doublet decorated with bands of gold braid; button fastening; short coat with full sleeves; padded breeches; slashed shoes. 2 English king *c.* 1541: flat hat with feather trim; short hair and cropped beard; undertunic decorated with tiny slashes; decorated codpiece; knee-length pleated skirt; garters; joined hose. 3 English queen *c.* 1545: small fabric headdress sewn with gold threads and edged with pearls; gown with low square neckline, trimmed with jewelled brooches; large fur cuffs; false undersleeves; split skirt; embroidered underskirt. 4 English prince *c.* 1547: hat trimmed with feathers and ruched ribbon; doublet, short coat and padded breeches trimmed with gold ribbons and braid.

5 French gentleman *c.* 1550: short coat with high standing collar, padded epaulettes and open hanging sleeves, all braided and edged with gold; padded breeches; large codpiece decorated with tiny slashes. 6 Italian official *c.* 1550: small felt hat; ankle-length coat with wide fur collar to hem and hanging sleeves; undergown buttoning at the front. 7 Spanish king *c.* 1550: black velvet hat with narrow brim and feather; doublet with standing collar and finely tucked bodice, the sleeves puffed, slashed and banded in tiers; puffed and padded breeches; leather shoes. 8 Italian lady *c.* 1550: brocade gown with puffed and slashed sleeves; gold mesh yoke embroidered with pearls; tight elongated bodice with tucked infill; skirt with brocade band, worn over pads and supporting frame.

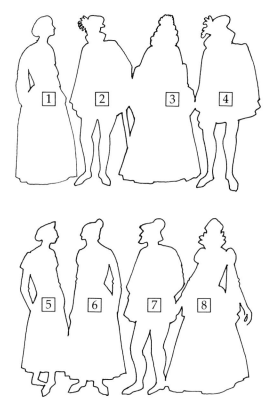

C. 1550

1 Italian lady: hair dressed in net scattered with pearls; brocade gown with square neckline; stiffly boned bodice; slashed sleeves pinned with brooches; skirt worn over pads and wire frame.
2 French king: velvet hat trimmed with pearls and white feather; short hair, pointed beard and small moustache; red velvet cape and tunic; padded breeches trimmed with gold braid; white hose; suede shoes with slashed decoration. 3 Italian princess: tiara embroidered with gold threads and pearls; gown with low square neckline; stiffened high lace collar; blue silk fabric embroidered with pearls; large fur cuffs; underskirt and false sleeves of pink silk.
4 Italian gentleman: velvet hat trimmed with feathers; coat with fur collar and gold braid, worn over the shoulders as cape; tight-fitting doublet; padded breeches worn with codpiece and hose.

5 Italian servant: linen cap; matching shawl tucked into laced bodice; ankle-length skirt; hose; mules. 6 English housemaid: transparent shawl; dress with laced bodice; linen apron. 7 Belgian peasant: hat with low brim; undertunic of coarse material; tunic with leather bindings; footless hose; leather shoes. 8 Italian lady: brocade gown with tight bodice; stiff, high lace collar; full skirt split at the front; hanging sleeves and hem trimmed with gold braid; waist-girdle.

C. 1551–1555

1 German gentleman c. 1551: velvet hat with narrow brim and feather decoration; fitted shoulder cape; standing collar; delicately embroidered tunic and padded breeches; slashed leather shoes.
2 German princess c. 1551: small stiffened beret with brooch and feather trim; floor-length coat with gold braid border; puffed and slashed sleeves in tiers; bodice of gown fastened with tiny bows and brooches. 3 Portuguese queen c. 1552: jewelled and embroidered headdress; gown with high collar edged with fine lace and worn under long coat; large puffed sleeves. 4 English queen c. 1554: small headdress edged with pearls; long veil; gown with high wing collar; tight bodice; turned-back cuffs; split skirt; brocade underskirt; belt; perfume bottle.

5 French lady c. 1555: tall, small-brimmed hat; lace-edged wing collar; shoulder cape decorated with gold braid; belt of tiny metal and pearl flowers; hem of gown and underskirt banded in gold.
6 Italian lady c. 1555: hair dressed into plaited braid; gown with low square neckline; pearl-scattered infill; large puffed and slashed sleeves; tight bodice; jewelled belt and matching necklace and earrings. 7 Spanish prince c. 1555: velvet hat trimmed with pearls and feathers; fur-lined, braid-trimmed cape with large wolf-fur edge; tunic with high collar; neck pendant; padded breeches. 8 Spanish gentleman c. 1555: hat with tall crown and padded brim; tunic with scalloped epaulettes, buttoning from neck to hem; geometric slashings and embroidery; slashed and scalloped leather shoes.

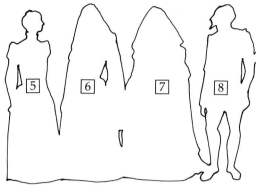

C. 1557–1560

1 French nobleman *c.* 1557: velvet hat with feather trim and jewelled band; short cloak, collar and shoulder cape with scalloped edges; braided and slashed tunic; padded breeches. 2 French gentleman *c.* 1558: velvet cap with feather trim and slashed decoration; short cloak, shoulder cape and collar with scalloped edges; slashed decoration on cloak, tunic, padded breeches and flat leather shoes. 3 Italian gentleman *c.* 1558: hat with tall crown and narrow brim topped by feather; short stamped-velvet coat with large padded and puffed upper sleeves; tight doublet; padded breeches; short leather boots. 4 Italian lady *c.* 1558: hair dressed over pads, decorated with brooch and long veil; high standing collar with frilled edge; brocade gown split at the front; tight bodice; long hanging sleeves decorated with braid and button fastenings.

5 German woman *c.* 1558: velvet gown with high standing collar; tight bodice; split skirt; small puffed sleeves; narrow wrist ruffs; chain belt. 6 Italian lady *c.* 1560: curled hair; long transparent veil; wide neck ruff and matching wrist ruffs; gown buttoning from neck to hem and trimmed with braid. 7 Italian lady *c.* 1560: long transparent veil attached to back of head and waist front; open neck ruff; tight bodice; short overskirt; brocade underskirt. 8 Spanish general *c.* 1560: narrow neck ruff; metal gorget and breastplate; padded breeches; leather shoes with instep strap.

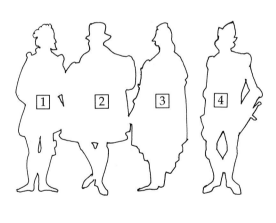

C. 1560

1 Spanish gentleman: cap with narrow brim and feather; neck and wrist ruffs; slashed tunic; padded epaulettes; breeches; green hose and wide fabric garters. 2 German councillor: hat with tall crown and narrow brim; fur-lined coat with large collar; slashed, padded and puffed sleeves. 3 Italian youth: small pill-box hat; long sleek hair; long cloak draped over one shoulder; padded sleeves of tunic decorated with looped ribbon. 4 Spanish soldier: engraved metal armour, including gorget, breastplate and jointed arm and leg protection; wide sash; fine cotton neck ruff.

5 Englishwoman: fine linen headdress and short veil; gown with high collar; tight bodice with yoke; full skirt worn over pads; waist-girdle. 6 German lady: hat with gathered crown and narrow brim; deep neck ruff; short jacket with large puffed sleeves; brocade gown worn over quilted underskirt. 7 Swedish king: short hair; long beard; hip-length coat with large puffed sleeves; doublet and breeches trimmed with gold embroidered panels; short leather boots. 8 German man: soft velvet hat with narrow stiffened brim; tunic with high collar; slashed bodice and sleeves; padded breeches.

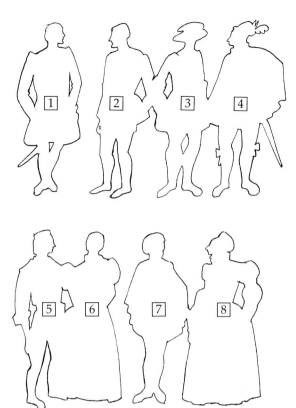

C. 1560–1565

1. Spanish man *c.* 1560: short hair and beard; tunic with high lace-edged collar, buttoning down the front; full padded breeches; ankle-shoes. 2. English groom *c.* 1560: brimless beret; undershirt; short coat with padded sleeves; codpiece and hose; leather shoes. 3. German baker *c.* 1560: stiff linen hat; undershirt of coarse material; tunic fastened with leather thongs; rolled-up sleeves; linen apron tied between the legs of padded breeches. 4. German man *c.* 1560: hat with tall crown, trimmed with feathers; high neck ruff; short cape; tunic with tight bodice, buttoning from neck to waist; padded breeches; ribbon garters tied in large bows.

5. Belgian countryman *c.* 1560: fabric hat; short shoulder cape and hood with scalloped edge; T-shaped tunic belted at the waist; hose; leather gaiters. 6. Spanish lady *c.* 1565: hair dressed over pads; deep neck ruff; long coat trimmed with gold braid; brocade undergown. 7. Italian man *c.* 1565: velvet beret; deep neck ruff; short cape fastened with brooch; tunic and matching breeches; hose; garters; flat shoes. 8. Italian gentlewoman *c.* 1565: sectioned cap trimmed with pearls and brooches; gown with fine lace collar; puffed and slashed sleeves; open skirt; jewelled belt.

C. 1565–1575

1. French gentleman *c.* 1565: velvet hat trimmed with feathers and brooches; short cape; tight-fitting tunic with deep skirt; neck chain and pendant; padded breeches; slashed shoes. 2. Flemish peasant *c.* 1565: linen turban and undershirt; tunic with leather thong fastenings; footless hose; laced leather ankle-boots. 3. English worker *c.* 1565: coarse linen turban and undershirt; large waist apron; knee-length hose; flat shoes. 4. French milkmaid *c.* 1565: linen bonnet and chin strap; coarse wool dress with rolled-up sleeves and bound hem, worn over two underdresses; long apron.

5. German gentleman *c.* 1570: hat with tall gathered crown and narrow brim; short coat with fur collar and lining, worn over the shoulders; stitched undertunic; deep neck ruff; fabric belt tied into large bow over codpiece; matching garters. 6. English statesman *c.* 1575: rectangular beret worn over skull cap; full-length robe with small train; deep fur collar; matching cuffs. 7. English butler *c.* 1575: tunic with padded epaulettes; deep neck ruff; padded breeches; waist apron. 8. English lady *c.* 1575: small tiara set with pearls and jewels; neck ruff; gown trimmed with pearls and brooches; low square neckline filled with gauze; padded epaulettes; tight bodice; open overskirt. 9. English queen *c.* 1575: tall-crowned hat trimmed with feathers; hair dressed in tight curls; velvet gown with low square neckline, tight bodice, open skirt; puffed and slashed sleeves decorated with bows.

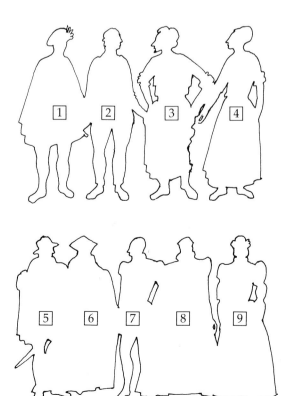

C. 1580

[1] Spanish princess: padded beret with pearl and feather trim; gown with high collar and stiffened frill; skirt worn over pads; open, hanging outer sleeves; tight bodice decorated with gold embroidery, brooches and pins; matching waist-girdle. [2] Italian man: tall hat with pleated crown and narrow brim; short cape with scalloped edge, worn over one shoulder; padded breeches; patterned hose. [3] German gentleman: hat with tall crown and wide brim, swathed in silk; wide neck ruff; tunic buttoning from neck to waist; epaulettes; bag sleeves; padded breeches with codpiece covered by large silk bow to match the garters. [4] Spanish lady: high lace-edged collar; velvet gown embroidered with gold thread; tight bodice ending in narrow peplum; full skirt over wire frame.

[5] Italian gentleman: hat with wide brim and feather trim; knee-length cape with large collar; tunic with flat linen collar; linen wrist ruffs; breeches gathered to knee. [6] Italian lady: net headdress trimmed with pearls; wired standing ruff; green dress with padded epaulettes; decorative hanging sleeves tied at back of skirt. [7] French gentleman: small velvet cap trimmed with brooch and feathers; large neck ruff with wire support; fitted tunic decorated with slashes and bands of velvet ribbon; short breeches with narrow slashes. [8] French gentleman: velvet cap with feather trim; short shoulder cape, tight tunic and knee-length breeches, all trimmed with gold lace.

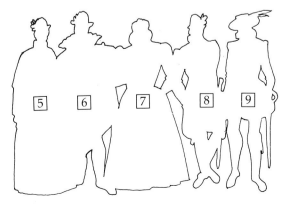

C. 1580–1590

[1] French countess c. 1580: jewelled headdress; hair dressed over pads; high neck ruff; gown with tight-fitting bodice; inset epaulettes; elbow-length oversleeves with deep embroidered cuffs; puffed and banded undersleeves; split skirt with ribbon tabs. [2] English royal guard c. 1580: black velvet beret trimmed with grey feather; red tunic with high standing collar; large puffed sleeves with velvet ribbon trim; matching wrapover skirt; gold embroidered bodice; short padded breeches. [3] English lady c. 1583: fine gauze headdress with pearl edge; wide wired ruff; gown with fitted bodice; large padded sleeves with ribbon trim; split skirt held by tiny bows to reveal embroidered skirt; folding feather fan at end of waist-girdle. [4] Spanish princess c. 1584: narrow-brimmed velvet cap trimmed with gold braid and feathers; gold- and pearl-embroidered floor-length coat with high wing collar; large puffed sleeves decorated with bows; fine leather gloves.

[5] Spanish princess c. 1585: tall-crowned hat with narrow brim; embroidered gown with fitted bodice and brooch trim; open sleeves pinned at elbow; full skirt split at the front and held together with ribbon tabs. [6] German courtier c. 1585: hat with tall stiffened crown and curled brim; short fur-trimmed cape; brooches pinned on tight tunic and large padded sleeves; padded breeches with codpiece covered by large silk bow to match garters. [7] Dutchwoman c. 1587: high neck ruff; patterned brocade gown with fitted bodice and full skirt; waist-girdle with pomander. [8] Spanish gentleman c. 1588: cloth-covered hat with tall crown and narrow brim; tunic worn with matching neck and wrist ruffs; knee-length breeches; silk garters; yellow hose. [9] English lord c. 1590: hat with shallow crown and wide brim; silver-trimmed tunic buttoning from neck to waist with long skirt; breeches; hose; shoes with ribbon bows.

C. 1590–1595

1 German man *c.* 1590: brimless hat trimmed with braid; full, unfitted, sleeveless tunic with padded epaulettes; neck and wrist ruffs; knee-length breeches. 2 German gentleman *c.* 1590: feather trim on hat with wide brim; tunic trimmed with gold braid; matching padded epaulettes; knee-breeches; silk garters and matching bow covering codpiece. 3 Swedish princess *c.* 1590: heart-shaped headdress studded with pearls and jewels; wide wire-framed ruff; gown with epaulettes, long hanging sleeves and fitted bodice; wide skirt worn over frame. 4 Italian man *c.* 1590: hat with narrow brim and soft crown; floor-length coat with high wing collar; knee-length undertunic of rich brocade; hose; garters; leather mules.

5 French servant *c.* 1590: linen cap; hip-length wool bodice with V-shaped neckline; coarse wool shirt; long linen apron; wool underskirt. 6 Italian lady *c.* 1590: curled hair decorated with jewelled brooch and long veil; gown with open hanging sleeves; short open overskirt; rich brocade underskirt. 7 English queen *c.* 1592: elaborately curled hair decorated with pins and brooches and topped with tiny crown; large flat lace ruff on wire-frame support; silk gown decorated with pins, jewelled brooches and pearls; wide skirt worn over cartwheel frame. 8 Venetian gentleman *c.* 1595: hat with tall crown and jewelled band; neck and wrist ruffs; tunic with slashed bodice and sleeves; large bow over codpiece; knee-length breeches.

C. 1595–1600

1 Spanish lady *c.* 1595: brimless hat with embroidered crown and feather trim; long coat with padded epaulettes; hanging sleeves with lace cuffs and gold braid to match undergown. 2 Spanish princess *c.* 1595: heart-shaped headdress edged with pearls; hair dressed into tight curls; gown with low square neckline filled with fine gauze; tight bodice, sleeves and skirt trimmed with rows of pearls.
3 German gentleman *c.* 1595–1598: tall-crowned hat with feather trim; fur-lined cape with high standing collar; tunic buttoning from neck to waist and worn with neck and wrist ruffs; large bow over codpiece; knee-length stockings worn over breeches and secured by narrow garters. 4 English soldier *c.* 1595–1597: metal armour, including helmet, breastplate and gauntlets, worn with short padded breeches.

5 Englishman *c.* 1598: wide-brimmed hat; tunic with epaulettes and flat lace collar, the front buttoning from neck to waist; narrow belt; short breeches with canions to the knee; brown hose; slashed shoes with wooden heels. 6 English countrywoman *c.* 1600: large hat worn over linen cap; coarse wool dress with white linen collar and cuffs; white linen apron. 7 English statesman *c.* 1600: embroidered cap; long gown with neck and wrist ruffs; embroidered hanging sleeves. 8 English lady *c.* 1600: hair dressed over pads; high wired lace collar and matching lace-edged cuffs; silk gown embroidered with sprigs of field flowers; ankle-length skirt worn over wide cartwheel frame; shoes with high wooden heels.

c. 1600-1606

English gentleman
c. 1600

Irishman
c. 1600

English
gentleman
c. 1602

English
gentleman
c. 1603

Englishwoman
c. 1605

English noblewoman
c. 1605

English noblewoman
c. 1605

English gentleman
c. 1606

English lady
c. 1610

Englishman
c. 1610

Dutchman
c. 1610

Dutch lady
c. 1610

English gentleman
c. 1610–1612

Dutch lady
c. 1612

English gentleman c. 1612

English gentleman c. 1613

C. 1613-1616

English nobleman
c. 1615

French gentleman
c. 1615

English
lady
c. 1615

English duchess
c. 1613–1615

English lord
c. 1616

English lady c. 1615

Dutch lady c. 1615

Englishwoman c. 1616

c. 1620-1629

English nobleman
c. 1620

English lady
c. 1622

English lady
c. 1625

English gentleman
c. 1625

English nobleman
c. 1626

English gentleman c. 1627

French gentleman c. 1629

French lady c. 1629

C. 1629-1635

Frenchman
c. 1629

English
gentleman
c. 1630

English lady
c. 1630

Italian man
c. 1630

English
military
gentleman
c. 1634

French lady c. 1630

French soldier c. 1635

English soldier c. 1635

c. 1635-1637

English lady
c. 1635

French lady
c. 1635

English gentleman
c. 1635

Spanish
princess
c. 1635

English lady
c. 1635

Englishman
c. 1637

English soldier c. 1635

French gentleman c. 1637

C. 1638-1641

Dutch kitchenmaid
c. 1638

Englishman
c. 1639

Dutch gentleman
c. 1640

English countrywoman
c. 1640

Dutch lady
c. 1640

English butcher
c. 1641

French gentleman c. 1640

Italian man c. 1640

c. 1641-1646

Dutchwoman
c. 1642

Italian man
c. 1642

English gentleman
c. 1641

English shepherd
c. 1642

English bishop c. 1645

English ratcatcher c. 1645

English gentleman c. 1646

English lady c. 1646

c. 1647-1650

Dutchman
c. 1647

Italian gentleman
c. 1648

Englishman
c. 1649

Italian farmer's
wife c. 1650

Italian farmer
c. 1650

Italian gentleman c. 1650

Dutch gentleman c. 1650

Dutch kitchenmaid c. 1650

c. 1655-1658

Englishwoman
c. 1655

English gentleman
c. 1655

English cobbler
c. 1655

English lady
c. 1655

Dutch gentleman
c. 1655

Dutch lady
c. 1656

German countrywoman c. 1655

Frenchwoman c. 1658

c. 1660-1665

Frenchman
c. 1660

French lady
c. 1660

Austrian queen
c. 1660

Dutchwoman
c. 1660

French king
c. 1660

French gentleman
c. 1660

French gentleman c. 1663

English
gentleman
c. 1665

c. 1665-1670

English lady
c. 1665

French gentleman
c. 1665

Spanish
noblewoman
c. 1665

French lady
c. 1670

Italian woman
c. 1670

French gentleman
c. 1665

English lady c. 1670

French lady c. 1670

c. 1670-1680

English
man-servant
c. 1670

French king
c. 1670

French lady
c. 1672

English
gentleman
c. 1675

English lady
c. 1677

French gentleman
c. 1678

Danish queen c. 1680

French lady c. 1680

c. 1680-1690

French gentleman
c. 1680

French lady
c. 1684

French
gentleman
c. 1685

French
Guards officer
c. 1685

French servant
c. 1690

French nobleman c. 1685

English gentleman c. 1689

French gentleman c. 1690

C. 1690-1695

French clergyman
c. 1690

French gentleman
c. 1690

English gentleman
c. 1692

English lady
c. 1692

French lady
c. 1694

English lady
c. 1695

French general c. 1694

French gentleman c. 1695

C. 1695-1700

German lady
c. 1695

French gentleman
c. 1695

Dutch
gentleman
c. 1695

Italian lady
c. 1695

French lady
c. 1698

French gentleman c. 1698

French gentleman c. 1698

English lady c. 1700

C. 1600–1606

[1] English gentleman *c.* 1600: wide-brimmed felt hat; padded doublet with flat lace collar and matching cuffs; padded breeches cut into panes; velvet canions to knee; fringed garters. [2] Irishman *c.* 1600: knee-length cape; tunic with high standing collar and short hand-stitched skirt; checked wool hose. [3] English gentleman *c.* 1602: tall hat with band and wide brim; knee-length coat; padded doublet with standing lace collar, the front buttoning from neck to waist; brocade breeches; thigh-length boots with small heels and spurs. [4] English gentleman *c.* 1603: embroidered doublet with epaulettes and short tabbed skirt; gathered breeches and matching canions; blue hose; high-heeled shoes with large rosettes.

[5] Englishwoman *c.* 1605: close-fitting velvet headdress and white undercap; gown with braided decoration and embroidered, ankle-length underskirt. [6] English noblewoman *c.* 1605: hair dressed over pads and decorated with feathers and flowers; gown with high standing lace collar supported on wire frame, long hanging sleeves and wide skirt on cartwheel frame; high-heeled slashed shoes with wired bows. [7] English noblewoman *c.* 1605: high standing lace collar on wire frame; low scooped neckline decorated with lace; sleeves adorned with jewelled brooches; stiff bodice; wide peplum; embroidered skirt worn over frame. [8] English gentleman *c.* 1606: tall hat with curled brim and feather trim; doublet with white linen collar and cuffs; braided wings, sleeves and breeches; silk sash garters; high-heeled shoes with large rosettes.

C. 1610–1613

[1] English lady *c.* 1610: hair dressed over pads and trimmed with single feather and flower; open ankle-length coat; embroidered gown with wide open-fronted sleeves held together by bows; low scooped neckline worn with infill and wide ruff; embroidered underskirt. [2] Englishman *c.* 1610: wide-brimmed hat with feather trim; doublet worn with unstarched ruff; full knee-breeches; leather shoes decorated with rosettes. [3] Dutchman *c.* 1610: close-fitting, brimless felt cap; plain doublet with wings and narrow tabs; gathered breeches; leather shoes. [4] Dutch lady *c.* 1610: delicate tiara of gold and pearls, trimmed with single feather; high pleated collar on wire support; gown with low scooped neckline edged with fine lace; deep ribbon-edged peplum over wide drum-shaped skirt.

[5] English gentleman *c.* 1610–1612: stiff felt hat with wide brim; embroidered doublet worn with ruff and flat lace collar; narrow tabs over short padded breeches and knee-length canions; silk garters; flat, slashed leather shoes. [6] Dutch lady *c.* 1612: starched and pleated standing collar; gown with low, scooped, lace-edged neckline and stiff bodice; peplum gathered over wide ankle-length skirt; shoes with high heels. [7] English gentleman *c.* 1612: knee-length coat with deep fur collar; padded epaulettes and hanging sleeves; doublet with lace collar and cuffs; shoes with wired bows. [8] English gentleman *c.* 1613: long cloak with deep fur collar and lace trimming; high lace-edged collar on wire support; embroidered doublet buttoning from neck to waist; brocade breeches; sash garters; high-heeled shoes with large rosettes.

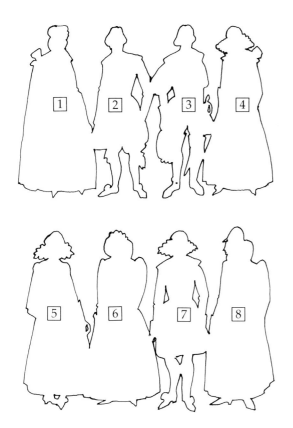

C. 1613–1616

1 English duchess *c.* 1613–1615: fine lace-edged cap; stole knotted over one shoulder; wide neck ruff; pearl necklaces; brocade gown with high neckline; long sleeves with lace cuffs; full skirt decorated with gold embroidery at the hem. 2 English nobleman *c.* 1615: doublet with wings, long sleeves and short tabs, decorated with tiny slashes; matching, gathered, knee-length breeches; sash garters; shoes with large rosettes. 3 French gentleman *c.* 1615: wide lace collar; doublet with tied tabs, buttoning from neck to waist; short gathered breeches; thigh-length boots worn with green canions. 4 English lady *c.* 1615: stole knotted over one shoulder; semi-circular collar supported on wire frame; gown with low scooped neckline edged with lace; three-quarter-length sleeves with wide lace cuffs; embroidered bodice and skirt.

5 English lady *c.* 1615: triangular lace cap; brocade overgown with epaulettes and hanging sleeves; ankle-length embroidered gown decorated with bows; high-heeled shoes with rosettes. 6 Dutch lady *c.* 1615: fine lace cap; large neck ruff; undergown buttoning from neck to low waist and trimmed with lace and borders of ribbon; feather fan; shoes with large rosettes. 7 English lord *c.* 1616: doublet with high standing collar, buttoning from the neck to the waist; short tabs; wrist-length sleeves with lace cuffs; jewelled waist-belt; gathered full breeches; high-heeled shoes. 8 Englishwoman *c.* 1616: tall-crowned hat with narrow brim, worn over lace undercap; wide ruff; sleeveless green coat; gown with tight-fitting bodice and gathered peplum.

C. 1620–1629

1 English nobleman *c.* 1620: lace collar and cuffs; embroidered doublet buttoning from neck to waist; jewelled waist-belt; gathered breeches; sash garters; high-heeled shoes with rosettes. 2 English lady *c.* 1622: lace cap; high falling collar; gown embroidered with flowers; low neckline with gauze infill; full skirt, the hem decorated with ribbon. 3 English lady *c.* 1625: hair dressed over pads, curled at fringe and decorated with ribbon; gown with lace-edged collars; wide elbow-length sleeves decorated with bows; large rosette under bust; high waist-belt; long stiffened busk; split skirt; embroidered underskirt; feather fan. 4 English gentleman *c.* 1625: wide-brimmed hat with tall crown and feather trim; doublet decorated with braid; slashed sleeves; deep tabs tied at high waist position; breeches with side buttons and knee bows.

5 English nobleman *c.* 1626: high lace collar; embroidered doublet; paned sleeves; tabs tied with ribbon bows; padded breeches; short matching canions; narrow garters; walking stick. 6 English gentleman *c.* 1627: long hair, moustache and small beard; doublet worn with unstarched ruff and lace cuffs; tabs tied with ribbons; gathered knee-length breeches; boot hose; bucket boots; boot leathers. 7 French gentleman *c.* 1629: hat decorated with feathers; long hair, moustache and small beard; cream-coloured falling collar; open tunic; slashed sleeves; long breeches; sash garters; high-heeled bucket boots with spurs. 8 French lady *c.* 1629: curled hair dressed over pads; starched standing collar; gown with low neckline; large sleeves decorated with bows; full skirt and underskirt worn over pads.

C. 1629–1635

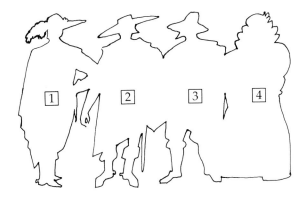

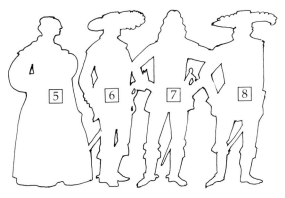

1 Frenchman *c.* 1629: wide-brimmed hat with feather trim; lace collar and cuffs; high-waisted doublet with tabs; matching knee-length breeches with button trim; bucket boots with boot leathers and spurs. 2 English gentleman *c.* 1630: cloak covered with tiny slashes; wide linen and lace falling collar; high-waisted doublet; matching knee-length breeches. 3 Italian man *c.* 1630: tall-crowned hat with wide band; long cloak wrapped around the waist and one shoulder; unstarched ruff; flat shoes. 4 English lady *c.* 1630: lace-edged standing collar; high-waisted gown in silk and velvet; long front busk; large padded sleeves with deep cuffs.

5 French lady *c.* 1630: silk gown with low neckline and lace trim: stiffened bodice trimmed with silk rosette; full skirt split in front. 6 English military gentleman *c.* 1634: hat trimmed with feathers; falling lace collar; leather doublet; sword belt; long breeches; bucket boots worn with boot hose, spurs and boot leathers. 7 French soldier *c.* 1635: long curled hair, moustache and small beard; green doublet worn with leather overtunic; slashed breeches; wide waist-sash and sword belt; bucket boots with butterfly boot leathers. 8 English soldier *c.* 1635: wide-brimmed hat trimmed with feathers; falling lace collar; breastplate worn over tunic with long skirt; sword belt; gauntlets; leather boots.

C. 1635–1637

1 English lady *c.* 1635: large hat with feather trim; long hair dressed into curls; wide falling lace collar; elbow-length puffed sleeves with lace cuffs; full skirt over petticoats. 2 French lady *c.* 1635: hair dressed into topknot and long side curls; low scooped neckline to edge of shoulders; double lace collar; high-waisted gown; sleeves with wide cuffs; split skirt; underskirt. 3 English gentleman *c.* 1635: large hat; long curled hair, moustache and short beard; doublet worn with lace-edged falling collar, paned sleeves and Spanish breeches; boot hose; long boots; butterfly boot leathers. 4 Spanish princess *c.* 1635: gold and pearl tiara; gown with low square neckline edged with lace and decorated with brooches; full puffed and slashed sleeves trimmed with pearls; deep lace cuffs; split skirt decorated with embroidery and pearls.

5 English soldier *c.* 1635: long curled hair, moustache and short beard; knee-length coat with linen collar; double sword belt; leather undercoat with wide silk sash; large hat with feather trim; leather bucket boots worn with butterfly boot leathers and spurs. 6 English lady *c.* 1635: large double lace collar; high-waisted gown with low square neckline; long busk; embroidered tabs; long gloves; feather fan. 7 Englishman *c.* 1637: falling collar and matching cuffs; doublet with short skirt, buttoning down the front; narrow waist-belt; Spanish breeches. 8 French gentleman *c.* 1637: feather-trimmed hat with wide brim; long cape; doublet with paned bodice and sleeves; Spanish breeches with ribbon trim; bucket boots worn with boot hose, butterfly boot leathers and clogs.

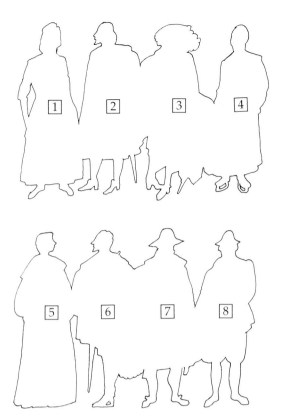

C. 1638–1641

1. Dutch kitchenmaid *c.* 1638: starched linen cap and matching collar; wool dress with laced front and rolled-up sleeves; linen apron. 2. Englishman *c.* 1639: knee-length cape; plain falling collar; doublet buttoning at the front; Spanish breeches; long boots with cuff, worn with boot hose, butterfly boot leathers and spurs. 3. Dutch gentleman *c.* 1640: large hat trimmed with feathers; unstarched ruff; brocade doublet with deep tabs; matching breeches; sash garters; red-heeled shoes with small rosettes. 4. English countrywoman *c.* 1640: linen cap; matching collar, cuffs and petticoat; short peplum skirt over wool skirt trimmed with embroidery; leather shoes on raised metal pattens.

5. Dutch lady *c.* 1640: shoulder cape and hood; silk mask; floor-length velvet coat trimmed with braid; fur muff. 6. French gentleman *c.* 1640: long hair curled and dressed into pigtails; wide lace collar; coat draped over one shoulder and trimmed with gold braid and buttons; fitted doublet; matching Spanish breeches; boots worn with butterfly boot leathers, spurs and clogs. 7. Italian man *c.* 1640: small fabric hat with gathered crown; long cloak with cape collar; neck ruff; doublet buttoning at the front; gathered breeches decorated with ribbons; sash garters; hose; leather shoes.
8. English butcher *c.* 1641: linen hat, collar, cuffs and short apron with large pocket; front-buttoning doublet with full skirt; gathered breeches; hose; leather shoes.

C. 1641–1646

1. English gentleman *c.* 1641: hat decorated with feathers; short cape with button fastening; wide lace-edged collar; doublet and long breeches in matching fabric, trimmed with braid; lace boot hose; bucket boots. 2. Dutchwoman *c.* 1642: hair dressed into ringlets and covered by small linen cap; matching linen collar; transparent undercollar; gown with fitted bodice and full skirt; three-quarter-length sleeves with wide linen cuffs. 3. Italian man *c.* 1642: hat with gathered crown; cloak with large collar; doublet with epaulettes and embroidered sleeves; knee-breeches; hose; leather shoes.
4. English shepherd *c.* 1642: wide-brimmed straw hat; linen collar and cuffs; tunic buttoning from neck to waist; wide leather belt holding hip bag; full gathered breeches; short hose pulled over long boots.

5. English bishop *c.* 1645: flat square-shaped hat worn over fitted skull cap; long surplice with full sleeves gathered into cuff; floor-length sleeveless coat; long blue stole. 6. English ratcatcher *c.* 1645: tall-crowned hat; doublet with wing collar and epaulettes, buttoning from neck to waist; leather belt and large bag; hose; sash garters. 7. English gentleman *c.* 1646: hat trimmed with feathers and ribbons; short tunic worn open; frilled shirt; wide, knee-length Spanish breeches decorated with frilled hem and ribbons at each side. 8. English lady *c.* 1646: hair dressed into side ringlets and decorated with ribbons and feathers; large double collar with lace trim; matching wide cuffs on three-quarter-length sleeves; fitted bodice; full skirt; feather fan.

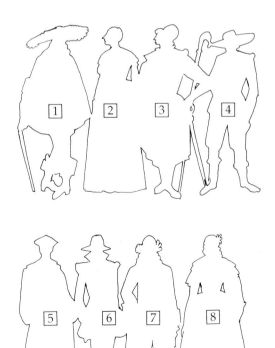

C. 1647–1650

⊡ Dutchman *c.* 1647: hat with tall crown and wide brim; linen falling collar and open cuffs; doublet buttoning down the front; gathered breeches. ⊡ Italian gentleman *c.* 1648: long hair, moustache and small beard; cloak worn over one shoulder; wide lace collar; fitted doublet buttoning from neck to waist; diagonal sword belt; full breeches tucked into boots; hat with feather trim. ⊡ Englishman *c.* 1649: hat with tall crown and wide brim; wide collar and cuffs; jacket buttoning from neck to hem; knee-length Spanish breeches; long leather boots with spurs. ⊡ Italian farmer's wife *c.* 1650: white linen headdress; short dress decorated with inset bands of contrasting colour and worn over long underskirt; large straw hat.

⊡ Italian farmer *c.* 1650: large straw hat with tall crown; cloak with short overcape and high collar, the hem decorated with embroidery; bound hose; ankle-boots. ⊡ Italian gentleman *c.* 1650: shoulder-length hair, moustache and small beard; short jacket with elbow-length sleeves and wide cuffs; full petticoat breeches; lace boot hose; long boots. ⊡ Dutch gentleman *c.* 1650: hat trimmed with feathers; long hair and moustache; shirt with lace collar; full sleeves visible under unbuttoned jacket sleeves; wide sash at high waist; long Spanish breeches; suede boots worn with butterfly boot leathers and spurs. ⊡ Dutch kitchenmaid *c.* 1650: hair dressed into bun; short jacket buttoning down the front; full skirt decorated at hem; apron; flat shoes.

C. 1655–1658

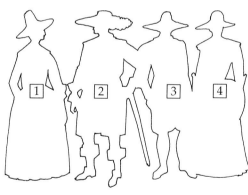

⊡ Englishwoman *c.* 1655: tall-crowned hat with wide brim, worn over white linen undercap; matching linen collar and cuffs; fitted bodice with peplum; three-quarter-length sleeves; full-length skirt gathered at waist. ⊡ English gentleman *c.* 1655: large-brimmed hat trimmed with feathers; embroidered tunic; linen shirt frilled at wrist and front of waist; wide embroidered knee-breeches; bucket boots with butterfly boot leathers; diagonal sword belt. ⊡ English cobbler *c.* 1655: wide-brimmed hat; coat with linen collar and cuffs; leather apron; breeches gathered at knee; hose; flat shoes. ⊡ English lady *c.* 1655: hat with tall crown and wide brim, worn over fine linen, lace-edged cap; matching double collar and cuffs on three-quarter-length sleeves; fitted bodice; overskirt looped up at each side of hip to reveal embroidered underskirt.

⊡ German countrywoman *c.* 1655: white linen cap with wide turned-back brim; bodice with deep scooped neckline; wide three-quarter-length sleeves with wide cuffs; gathered skirt decorated with ribbon bands; large apron; undergown visible at neck and lower arm. ⊡ Dutch gentleman *c.* 1655: hat with upturned brim, trimmed with feathers; neck cloth; long coat worn open at the front; ribbon decoration on right shoulder; elbow-length sleeves with deep cuffs; long waistcoat; diagonal sword belt; breeches gathered at knee; bucket boots with high heels; embroidered gauntlets. ⊡ Dutch lady *c.* 1656: linen cap, collar and cuffs with stitched detail; fitted bodice with bound seams; short overskirt cut into points; underskirt trimmed with braid. ⊡ Frenchwoman *c.* 1658: linen bonnet tied under chin; fitted bodice; skirt looped up at the front; short sleeves; linen petticoat.

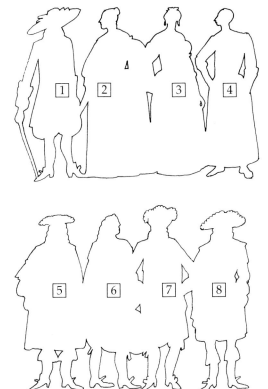

C. 1660–1665

[1] Frenchman *c.* 1660: wide-brimmed hat with looped ribbons; shoulder-length hair; long coat buttoned to waist with hip-level pockets; elbow-length sleeves with wide cuffs; full breeches gathered at knee; shoes with high heels, high tongues and wired ribbon bows. [2] French lady *c.* 1660: hair dressed into bun and long side ringlets; gown with wide neckline to tip of shoulders; draped silk secured with brooches; full sleeves gathered into band at elbow; peplum; full skirt with braided hem. [3] Austrian queen *c.* 1660: drop earrings and matching pearl necklace; wide collar decorated with brooches; tight-fitting bodice ending in peplum; short sleeves with decorative bows; long gloves; full skirt split at the front to reveal embroidered underskirt. [4] Dutchwoman *c.* 1660: embroidered cap tied under chin; fitted bodice with deep peplum; three-quarter-length sleeves with cuffs; undergown; large apron.

[5] French king *c.* 1660: small hat covered with feathers and tiny bows; wide lace-edged collar and neck cloth; short jacket with short sleeves; full shirt gathered at waist and wrist; overskirt decorated with looped ribbons; hose with lace frill over knee. [6] French gentleman *c.* 1660: shoulder-length wig; coat with high yoke and short sleeves, decorated with looped ribbon; gathered breeches; shoes with high red heels and wired bows; large hat trimmed with feathers. [7] French gentleman *c.* 1663: hat with large feather trim; long curled wig; short jacket; linen shirt; loops of ribbon ties at waist; breeches; high-heeled shoes; diagonal sword belt. [8] English gentleman *c.* 1665: feather-trimmed hat with brim, turned up at front and back; short jacket; petticoat breeches; hose with frill at knee; shoes with high heels and wired bow decoration.

C. 1665–1670

[1] English lady *c.* 1665: pearl necklace; gown of striped silk, the fitted bodice with low neckline and lace-edged collar; large brooch set with pearls; gathered skirt split at the front to reveal dark underskirt. [2] French gentleman *c.* 1665: hat with tall crown, trimmed with feathers; long cloak; neck cloth; short embroidered jacket; shirt with full sleeves gathered into frill at wrist; full petticoat breeches to the knee with ribbon trim; hose with lace frill. [3] Spanish noblewoman *c.* 1665: shoulder-length hair with rosette decoration; fitted bodice with low neckline and embroidered collar; large gathered sleeves trimmed with bows; embroidered skirt split at the front to reveal underskirt. [4] French gentleman *c.* 1665: hat with small upturned brim and feather trim; shoulder-length wig; cravat with bow decoration; long coat with waist-sash; gathered sleeves trimmed with ribbon; gathered breeches; lace frill at knee; hose; shoes with high red heels, high tongues and wired bows.

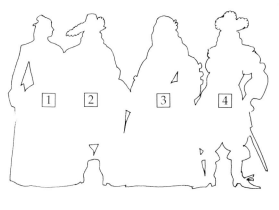

[5] French lady *c.* 1670: hair dressed into curls and bun; gown with fitted bodice and low neckline, the sleeves gathered at elbow length into cuff; overskirt split at the front and tied back with bows on each side. [6] Italian woman *c.* 1670: cap with gathered edge and back streamers; fitted bodice laced at the front; gathered skirt. [7] English lady *c.* 1670: gown of fine embroidered silk with wide off-the-shoulder neckline; puffed and tiered sleeves; overskirt split at the front and tied at the sides over plain underskirt. [8] French lady *c.* 1670: gown with wide off-the-shoulder neckline and fitted bodice; puffed sleeves trimmed with bows; gathered skirt looped at back waist to give long train; underskirt trimmed with braid ribbon and fringing.

C. 1670–1680

1 English man-servant *c.* 1670: wide-brimmed hat; neck cloth tied into bow; hip-length coat buttoning down the front; narrow belt; knee-length breeches; hose; flat-heeled shoes. 2 French king *c.* 1670: small hat with narrow brim and rosette and feather trim; shoulder-length curled wig; neck cloth; matching shirt, cuffs and garters; short jacket with short sleeves; matching overskirt; full breeches; red-heeled shoes decorated with bows and rosettes. 3 French lady *c.* 1672: neckline edged with lace to match frilled cuff; fitted bodice; overskirt split and looped up at each side; underskirt trimmed with lace. 4 English gentleman *c.* 1675: hat with tall crown and wide brim; neck cloth tied into bow; knee-length coat with short sleeves; long waistcoat; breeches gathered at knee; garters; shoes with red heels, high tongues and wide bows.

5 English lady *c.* 1677: gown with scooped neckline; fitted bodice, the central panel decorated with silk rosettes; elbow-length sleeves with embroidered cuffs; overskirt looped up at back; lace-trimmed underskirt. 6 Danish queen *c.* 1680: fontange of pleated and stiffened lace worn over frilled cap; gown with low square neckline; velvet bodice, sleeves, and back skirt train trimmed with lace and ribbon; fur muff decorated with large ribbon bow. 7 French gentleman *c.* 1678: large hat trimmed with ribbons and feathers; long curled wig; neck cloth; fitted knee-length coat; three-quarter-length cuffed sleeves; fringed sash; gathered breeches; garters with large bows. 8 French lady *c.* 1680: high fontange of stiffened lace covered with silk scarf; mask; gown of striped silk, the bodice with low square neckline; lace apron; small muff with bow decoration.

C. 1680–1690

1 French gentleman *c.* 1680: wide-brimmed hat with ribbon and feather trim; lace neck cloth and stiffened bow; long cape with wide embroidered border; matching fitted coat; small fur muff with bow decoration; knee-length stockings; garters; shoes with high red heels and extended tongues. 2 French lady *c.* 1684: headdress of fine stiffened ribbon; silk scarf; boned bodice decorated with looped ribbons; open skirt looped up at each side; embroidered underskirt; long gloves. 3 French gentleman *c.* 1685: shoulder-length curled wig; silk cravat; knee-length, fitted brocade coat; waistcoat; wide sash; hat with feather trim; long walking stick. 4 French Guards officer *c.* 1685: feather-trimmed hat; long curled wig; knee-length, fitted brocade coat; diagonal embroidered sash; gauntlets; gathered breeches; hose; high-heeled shoes.

5 French nobleman *c.* 1685: large hat trimmed with curled feathers; long curled wig; fitted coat with wide cuffs, worn over long waistcoat; fur muff fastened to waist-sash; hose; knee-garters; high-heeled shoes; walking stick. 6 English gentleman *c.* 1689: shoulder-length wig; lace-edged silk neck cloth; matching shirt cuffs; fitted coat with flared skirt, low pockets and embroidered cuffs; knee-breeches; stockings; shoes with high tongues. 7 French servant *c.* 1690: linen turban; cape collar; bodice laced at the front; ankle-length skirt; apron; flat leather shoes. 8 French gentleman *c.* 1690: long curled wig; neck cloth with lace trim; long fitted coat, the seams trimmed with fur; brocade waistcoat; leather gauntlets; stockings with embroidered clocks.

C. 1690–1695

[1] French clergyman c. 1690: hat with shallow crown and wide brim; falling band; fitted coat with full skirt; fur muff fastened to waist-sash. [2] French gentleman c. 1690: hat with upturned brim and feather and ribbon trim; long curled wig; lace neck cloth and stiff ribbon bow; fitted coat with full skirt and low-placed pockets, the wide-cuffed sleeves decorated with buttons; long waistcoat; breeches; ribbon garters. [3] English gentleman c. 1692: long curled wig; face patch; neck cloth; fitted coat with full skirt and button and braid detail; long waistcoat buttoning from neck to hem; gathered breeches; narrow garters; hose; high-heeled shoes. [4] English lady c. 1692: wired headdress; hair dressed into formal curls; face patches; pearl drop earrings; matching single strand of pearls; gown with wide neckline; fitted bodice decorated with rosettes; short sleeves with wide cuffs; chemise; skirt split and held at the back; underskirt in matching fabric.

[5] French lady c. 1694: high fontange; hair dressed over pads; pearl necklace; gown with boned bodice; underskirt trimmed with lace, braid and fringing. [6] French general c. 1694: hat with shallow crown and wide brim, trimmed with single feather; long wig; knee-length fitted coat with contrasting colour facings and gold buttons; long waistcoat worn under breastplate; wide sash; long boots and spurs. [7] English lady c. 1695: cap and wired frill; face patch; gown with short sleeves, the bodice tight and the skirt full; decorative apron; embroidered underskirt. [8] French gentleman c. 1695: hat with upturned brim and feather trim; fitted knee-length coat with low pockets; long waistcoat buttoning down the front; breeches; high-heeled shoes.

C. 1695–1700

[1] Italian lady c. 1695: high, stiff lace frill worn over small cap; embroidered shawl; fitted bodice; elbow-length sleeves with cuffs; split skirt forming long train; underskirt in matching fabric. [2] German lady c. 1695: fontange of ribbon and lace; gown with wide neckline worn off the shoulder; brooch decoration on sleeves; cuffs with double-lace frill; fur muff with bow; embroidered and fringed underskirt. [3] French gentleman c. 1695: hat with fur-trimmed brim; long curled hair; fitted coat with three-quarter-length sleeves and wide cuffs; cravat of plain silk; shirt worn over fitted breeches; knee-stockings; narrow ribbon garters. [4] Dutch gentleman c. 1695: short curled wig with side ringlets; face patch; fitted coat with full skirt; cravat tucked into waistcoat; second waistcoat; breeches with pockets; knee-stockings; high-heeled leather shoes.

[5] French gentleman c. 1698: long curled wig; neck cloth and stiffened ribbon bow; fitted coat with large cuffs; fur muff on cord around neck; tricorn hat; narrow breeches; shoes with square toes and high heels. [6] French lady c. 1698: hair dressed into formal curls with long ringlets at back; fitted bodice trimmed with satin bows; full open skirt tied at the sides; underskirt decorated with ribbons and fringing. [7] French gentleman c. 1698: fitted coat buttoning from neck to hem; ribbon decoration worn on right shoulder; narrow sleeves with wide cuffs; tricorn hat. [8] English lady c. 1700: tricorn hat; shoulder-length hair; masculine-style riding coat with open front and full skirt; lace neck cloth; underskirt with deep hem frill.

c. 1700-1715

German court
lady c. 1700

English lady
c. 1700

English lady
c. 1705

English
gentleman
c. 1711

English lady
c. 1712

English gentleman
c. 1710

English lady c. 1712

English gentleman c. 1715

C. 1717-1729

French
gentleman
c. 1717

English gentleman
c. 1720

German gentleman
c. 1720

English lady c. 1718

English parlourmaid
c. 1720

French court lady
c. 1728

English lady c. 1720

Dutch gentleman c. 1729

c. 1730-1735

French lady
c. 1730

German gentleman
c. 1731

German lady
c. 1731

French lady
c. 1733

English lady
c. 1735

French lady c. 1735   English middle-class lady c. 1735   English lady c. 1735

C. 1740-1745

Italian gentleman
c. 1740

English parlourmaid
c. 1743

French lady
c. 1745

English lady
c. 1745

Venetian lady c. 1745

English cavalry officer c. 1745

English gentleman
c. 1745

French gentleman c. 1745

c. 1750

English countrywoman

English lady

English dandy

French flower seller

French lady

American middle-class lady

English gentleman

French lady

133

c. 1755-1765

American working man c. 1755

American maid c. 1755

English clergyman c. 1760

French court lady c. 1759

English gentleman c. 1760

French gentleman c. 1765

French lady c. 1762

Spanish noblewoman c. 1765

c. 1770

English maid

French lady

French servant

English countryman

English lady

American Quaker woman

Prussian army officer

American merchant

C. 1775-1777

English middle-class lady
c. 1775

English gentleman
c. 1775

French court lady
c. 1775

Englishwoman c. 1775

English lady
c. 1775

French noblewoman
c. 1777

French lady c. 1775

French court lady c. 1776

C. 1777-1780

French court lady
c. 1777

French lady
c. 1778

American lady
c. 1778

Italian lady
c. 1779

French lady
c. 1780

French lady
c. 1780

French lady c. 1779

Dutch court lady c. 1780

English gentleman
c. 1780

English gentleman c. 1781

American
gentleman
c. 1785

French court lady c. 1785

American
gentleman
c. 1785

French lady
c. 1785

French noblewoman
c. 1785

English lady c. 1785

C. 1785

English lady

French lady

English nobleman

Swedish lady

French lady

English gentleman

English lady

French lady

C. 1786-1788

French courtier
c. 1786

French courtier
c. 1786

French lady
c. 1787

English lady
c. 1788

French gentleman
c. 1788

French gentleman
c. 1788

French lady c. 1788   French gentleman c. 1788

140

c. 1790

French gentleman

English lady

French lady

English lady

French gentleman

French lady

English cook

American gentleman

141

C. 1790

French lady

French gentleman

French lady

French gentleman

French lady

French gentleman

French lady

French lady

C. 1791-1796

French lady c. 1791

French gentleman
c. 1791

French gentleman

French lady
c. 1791

c. 1792

French gentleman
c. 1792

French lady
c. 1795

French gentleman c. 1792

Young French gentleman c. 1796

C. 1796-1799

French gentleman
c. 1796

Young French gentleman
c. 1796

Spanish noblewoman
c. 1798

Young French
gentleman
c. 1798

French gentleman
c. 1799

Young French lady
c. 1799

Young French lady c. 1799

French lady c. 1799

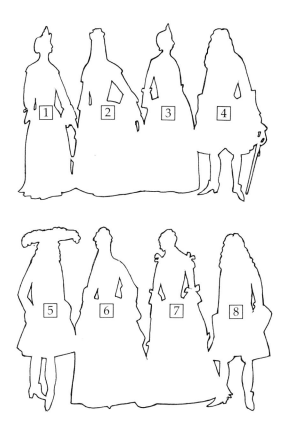

C. 1700–1715

[1] German court lady *c.* 1700: gauze bonnet with stiffened lace frill, trimmed with silk ribbons; gown with wide neckline, lace collar and fitted bodice; skirt split at the front; long train looped up with lace.
[2] English lady *c.* 1700: stiffened lace headdress; lace veil; gown with fitted bodice trimmed with bows and brooches; sleeves with pleated cuff and lace frill; full underskirt worn over pads and stiff petticoats, looped up at each side. [3] English lady *c.* 1705: small cap with stiffened frill; gown with fitted bodice trimmed with bows, the skirt looped up at each side; silk underskirt. [4] English gentleman *c.* 1711: shoulder-length wig; cravat with lace edge; matching frilled shirt cuffs; knee-length coat with gold braid trimming and low pockets; brocade waistcoat; silk stockings; shoes with red heels.

[5] English gentleman *c.* 1710: tricorn hat with feather trim; knee-length velvet coat trimmed with gold braid, with large cuffs and low pockets; fur muff. [6] English lady *c.* 1712: cap with stiffened and pleated lace frill; striped silk gown with fitted bodice; skirt looped up at each side; silk underskirt; fine silk gauze apron embroidered with flowers. [7] English lady *c.* 1712: curled hair with ringlets; gown with low scooped neckline; bodice trimmed with jewelled brooches; full skirt worn over hip pads and stiffened petticoats; folding fan.
[8] English gentleman *c.* 1715: velvet coat trimmed with gold braid; knee-length brocade waistcoat; velvet breeches; shoes with silver buckles.

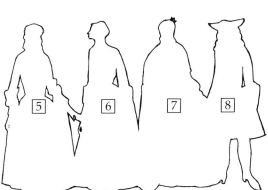

C. 1717–1729

[1] French gentleman *c.* 1717: long curled wig; velvet coat buttoning from neck to hem; wide cuffs faced in contrasting colour and fabric; lace-edged cravat and matching frilled cuffs; long waistcoat; velvet breeches; silk stockings. [2] English lady *c.* 1718: small cap with frill and ribbon trim; striped silk gown embroidered with flowers; sacque back and train. [3] English gentleman *c.* 1720: long brown wig; fitted flared coat with deep cuffs; striped silk waistcoat; silk stockings worn over velvet breeches, secured by narrow garters; leather shoes.
[4] German gentleman *c.* 1720: long wig powdered grey; lace-edged cravat; fitted coat; tricorn hat trimmed with feathers; brocade waistcoat; silk stockings worn over velvet breeches; high-heeled leather shoes.

[5] English lady *c.* 1720: hair dressed under lace cap with frilled edge and long ribbon ends; gown with three-quarter-length sleeves; bodice and sleeves decorated with loops of ribbon, lace and pleating; fine gauze false undersleeves and frill; decorative apron. [6] English parlourmaid *c.* 1720: linen cap with band and frilled edge; matching cuffs, apron and fichu. [7] French court lady *c.* 1728: hair decorated with feathers and flowers, dressed over a pad and into side ringlets; floor-length cape worn over silk gown and underskirt. [8] Dutch gentleman *c.* 1729: tricorn hat; long wig; lace-edged stock; knee-length velvet coat; long waistcoat; velvet knee-breeches; high-heeled boots.

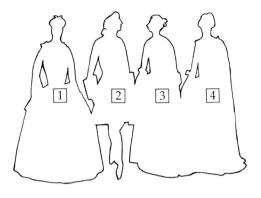

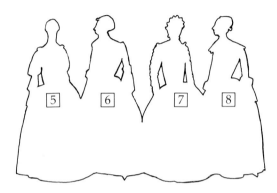

C. 1730–1735

1 French lady *c.* 1730: cap decorated with ribbon bow; gown with pierrot bodice and flared sleeves; false undersleeves and frill; full skirt worn over panniers. 2 German gentleman *c.* 1731: powdered wig tied back into large bow; fitted coat with flared skirt; braid and bow trimming on coat, wide cuffs, side openings and pockets; brocade waistcoat with buttons in sets of two. 3 German lady *c.* 1731: small cap trimmed with bow; hair dressed into plaited bun; embroidered gown with three-quarter-length, lace frilled sleeves; sacque back with deep centre pleat; small train. 4 French lady *c.* 1733: hair dressed into tight curls; gown in flower and leaf pattern with scooped neckline frilled at edge; fitted bodice; skirt worn over panniers; sacque back; small train.

5 French lady *c.* 1735: hair powdered and decorated with tiny flowers; gown with wide, scooped, ruched neckline; fitted bodice decorated with a series of pleated fabric fan shapes; full skirt worn over panniers. 6 English middle-class lady *c.* 1735: gauze cap with frilled edge; gown with fitted bodice; sleeves with cuffs and lace frill; full skirt; transparent fichu and apron. 7 English lady *c.* 1735: cap with gathered lace frill; gown with fitted bodice; sleeves with ruched and pleated detail; full skirt split at the front to reveal quilted underskirt. 8 English lady *c.* 1735: cap with frilled edge; lace shoulder cape and sleeve frill; gown of patterned silk with front-laced fitted bodice and full skirt.

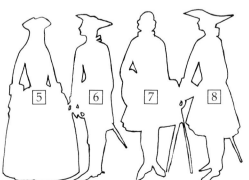

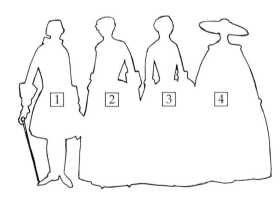

C. 1740–1745

1 Italian gentleman *c.* 1740: powdered wig dressed into formal side curls; matching coat and waistcoat trimmed with contrasting colour and gold braid; velvet knee-breeches; silk stockings; leather shoes. 2 English parlourmaid *c.* 1743: cap with frilled edge, tied under the chin with ribbon; dress with fitted bodice and three-quarter-length sleeves; fichu with frilled edge; full skirt looped up at one side; long apron. 3 French lady *c.* 1745: powdered and padded hair; pearl necklace; gown with fitted bodice decorated with large bows; tight sleeves with wide frill from elbow; skirt with embroidered underskirt worn over panniers. 4 English lady *c.* 1745: walking costume: short fur-trimmed pelisse and matching fur muff; wide-brimmed hat and underbonnet; long apron with deep frill.

5 Venetian lady *c.* 1745: travelling costume: masculine tricorn hat worn over lace veil; gown with fitted bodice with button decoration; tight sleeves with wide cuffs; split skirt and underskirt worn over panniers. 6 English cavalry officer *c.* 1745: tricorn hat trimmed with gold braid; wig with long pigtail; knee-length coat split at the back; high cuffed boots worn with boot leathers and spurs. 7 English gentleman *c.* 1745: wig dressed into formal side curls and tied back with large bow; fitted knee-length coat with flared skirt, trimmed with gold braid; fur muff. 8 French gentleman *c.* 1745: large tricorn hat; powdered wig tied back with large bow; hair held in bag; long fitted coat with flared skirt; breeches; silk stockings; leather shoes with low heels.

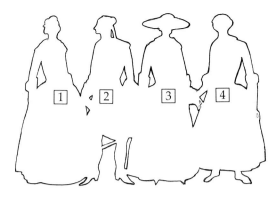

C. 1750

1 English lady: lace-edged cap; fichu trimmed with large silk bow; silk gown with fitted bodice; full skirt worn over stiff petticoats; elbow-length sleeves with cuffs and lace frills. 2 English dandy: powdered wig tied back with large bow and ending in long plait; knee-length coat with flared skirt, buttoning from neck to hem; large fur muff; walking stick tied with ribbons. 3 English country-woman: wide-brimmed hat worn over mob cap; fichu; dress with front-laced bodice; three-quarter-length sleeves with cuffs and false undersleeves; full skirt; linen apron. 4 French flower seller: mob cap; ankle-length dress with fitted bodice and full skirt; linen scarf and bib apron.

5 French lady: neck frill; ballgown with deep scooped neckline frilled at edge; fitted bodice with embroidered front panel and matching decoration on full skirt worn over stiff petticoats and panniers. 6 American middle-class lady: wide-brimmed straw hat worn over frilled lingerie cap and tied under the chin with ribbons; fine fichu of spotted gauze; dress with fitted bodice and full skirt split at the front, worn with quilted petticoat and bib apron. 7 English gentleman: tricorn hat braided at edge; brown wig; stock bound high around neck; fitted knee-length coat; waistcoat; velvet breeches. 8 French lady: hair decorated with tiny wax flowers; embroidered silk gown with wide sacque back with deep box pleat; long train.

C. 1755–1765

1 American working man c. 1755: wide-brimmed hat; muslin cravat; long coat buttoning from neck to hem; short waistcoat; breeches; striped stockings. 2 American maid c. 1755: mob cap tied under chin; lawn fichu; striped top with three-quarter-length sleeves; ankle-length skirt; linen bib apron; pattens with wooden soles.
3 French court lady c. 1759: hair decorated with wax flowers; frilled neck ribbon and bow; gown with low square neckline; fitted bodice and pagoda sleeves decorated with bows and lace frills; skirt supported on panniers; underskirt trimmed with ruching and frills.
4 English clergyman c. 1760: wig with side curls; white cravat and clerical bands; fitted coat buttoning to waist; breeches; garters; stockings; shoes.

5 English gentleman c. 1760: powdered wig; muslin cravat; fitted coat with matching waistcoat and breeches; silk stockings; shoes with low heels. 6 French gentleman c. 1765: powdered wig tied back with large bow; lace-trimmed lawn stock with matching wrist frills; velvet coat trimmed with gold braid; short brocade waistcoat; tight breeches with buttons on knee; silk stockings with clocks.
7 French lady c. 1762: powdered wig with side ringlets and pearl decoration; gown with low square neckline and fitted bodice, trimmed with ribbons, bows and ruffles; polonaise skirt over frilled underskirt. 8 Spanish noblewoman c. 1765: hair dressed with wide plait; neck frill with bow; embroidered gown with wide neckline edged with wax flowers and bows; fitted sleeves with very deep cuffs; skirt supported on wide panniers.

C. 1770

1 English maid: small frilled mob cap; white muslin fichu and sleeve frill; dress with fitted bodice and three-quarter-length cuffed sleeves; full skirt. 2 French lady: wide-brimmed straw hat worn over muslin bonnet; embroidered sacque-back gown trimmed with ruched fabric and ribbon. 3 French servant: pleated bonnet; cotton fichu, apron and sleeve frills; dress with ankle-length skirt; leather shoes; metal pattens. 4 English countryman: wide-brimmed straw hat; spotted neck scarf; hip-length coat buttoning from neck to hem; small collar; short waistcoat; knee-breeches; cotton stockings; leather shoes.

5 English lady: powdered wig decorated with ribbons; gown with low scooped neckline, fitted bodice and three-quarter-length sleeves; false undersleeves to wrist; skirt draped over self-fabric underskirt. 6 American Quaker woman: lawn cap fastening under chin; cotton scarf crossed over at the front and tied at the back; high-waisted apron; skirt worn without hoops or stiffened petticoats. 7 Prussian army officer: tricorn hat trimmed with braid; powdered wig; coat with high collar and wide revers, cut short at front and with long tails at back; short waistcoat and matching breeches; sash with fringed ends; knee-length boots. 8 American merchant: dark wig tied back with ribbon bow; long coat with high collar and deep cuffs; hip-length waistcoat; knee-breeches; leather shoes with low heels and silver buckles.

C. 1775–1777

1 English middle-class lady *c. 1775*: tiny muslin cap trimmed with bow; neck ribbon; gown with low square neckline edged with pleated frill; embroidered bodice, sleeves and looped-up skirt; satin underskirt with quilted hem. 2 English gentleman *c. 1775*: tricorn hat; powdered wig; coat with high standing collar; narrow sleeves with small cuffs; long silk waistcoat; striped knee-breeches.
3 French court lady *c. 1775*: high powdered wig topped with feathers and flowers; gown with low neckline, fitted bodice, pagoda sleeves and looped-up skirt, trimmed with pleated bows, cords and tassels; skirt and underskirt supported with panniers.
4 Englishwoman *c. 1775*: straw hat trimmed with bows, worn over muslin bonnet; cotton fichu, false sleeves and waist apron; painted, striped linen gown with high neckline and ankle-length skirt.

5 French lady *c. 1775*: hat with upturned brim, trimmed with loops of ribbon; high powdered wig; gown of silk and spotted muslin with ruching and ribbon decoration. 6 English lady *c. 1775*: powdered wig; large turban; gown with low neckline filled with fine muslin; bodice and sleeves trimmed with large taffeta bows. 7 French court lady *c. 1776*: large hat trimmed with feathers, loops of ribbon and large bows; powdered wig; gown with scooped neckline and sleeves decorated with pearls. 8 French noblewoman *c. 1777*: powdered wig decorated with wax flowers and tall feathers; corsage of wax flowers; gown with low scooped neckline and pagoda sleeves; delicate embroidery on skirt and hem of matching underskirt.

C. 1777–1780

[1] French court lady *c.* 1777: powdered wig topped with feathers; pearl necklace; pearl-trimmed gown with low neckline edged with bows; tight bodice; narrow sleeves with deep cuffs; wide skirt.
[2] French lady *c.* 1778: walking costume: hat with upturned brim and feather trim; knee-length pelisse lined and trimmed with fur; matching muff. [3] American lady *c.* 1778: ruffled lawn cap with ribbon trim, tied under chin; sacque-back gown with embroidered bodice and skirt and ruched ribbon trim. [4] Italian lady *c.* 1779: square of gauze fabric over powdered wig; gown with low square neckline; fitted bodice and pagoda sleeves trimmed with large taffeta bows; full skirt worn over panniers.

[5] French lady *c.* 1779: travelling costume: large hat with pleated brim and looped ribbon decoration; redingote in embroidered striped silk with velvet collar and cuffs, buttoning from neck to hem; walking stick; leather gloves. [6] French lady *c.* 1780: riding costume: hat with tall crown and wide brim; long dark wig; double-breasted velvet redingote with collar and cuffs in contrasting colour; voile fichu and gown. [7] French lady *c.* 1780: afternoon dress: small cap trimmed with pleating and ribbon; gauze scarf; painted, ankle-length gown with sacque back looped up at one side; high-heeled silk shoes. [8] Dutch court lady *c.* 1780: wig powdered and decorated with small wax flowers; neck frill; gown with low square neckline and tight elbow-length sleeves with double lace frill; wide skirt over panniers.

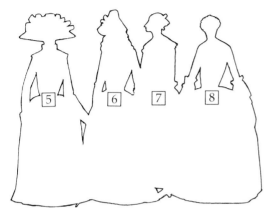

C. 1780–1785

[1] English gentleman *c.* 1780: powdered wig; silk stock; brocade coat with high collar, trimmed with braid; long matching waistcoat; velvet knee-breeches; silk stockings; leather shoes. [2] English gentleman *c.* 1781: walking costume: hat with small crown and wide upturned brim; double-breasted coat with full skirt and quilted collar and cuffs; walking stick; silk stockings with embroidered clocks.
[3] American gentleman *c.* 1785: powdered wig; stock and large bow; short double-breasted waistcoat; coat cut short at the front and into tails at the back; knee-breeches; long leather boots; boot leathers and spurs. [4] French court lady *c.* 1785: powdered wig worn with large draped turban; pearl necklace; silk gown, the neckline edged with lace frills; fine embroidered apron.

[5] American gentleman *c.* 1785: tall hat with hatband and narrow curled brim; coat with long tails; short double-breasted waistcoat; tight knee-breeches; long leather boots with deep cuff. [6] French noblewoman *c.* 1785: powdered wig with long ringlets; deep lace-edged scarf; gown with full skirt and petticoats trimmed with bands of ruching. [7] French lady *c.* 1785: walking costume: hat with tall crown and wide brim, trimmed with ribbon and feathers; long wig; fine gauze scarf tucked into wide waist-sash; two watch fobs; embroidered redingote. [8] English lady *c.* 1785: summer walking costume: wide-brimmed hat trimmed with ribbons and feathers; finely striped muslin gown; semi-transparent scarf and stole; fine leather gloves.

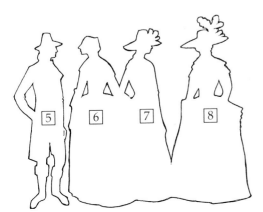

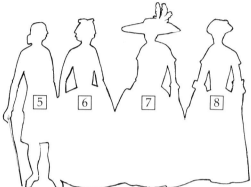

C. 1785

1 English lady: large hat trimmed with loops of ribbon and feathers; long curled wig; muslin fichu; silk gown with ribbon trimming; large fur muff with silk bow. 2 French lady: riding costume: feather-trimmed tricorn; fitted jacket with velvet revers, short peplum and full skirt; silk shoes with bow trim. 3 English nobleman: powdered wig with side curls; embroidered coat and matching waistcoat; knee-breeches; garters; silk stockings with embroidered clocks. 4 Swedish lady: powdered wig with feather decoration; silk high-necked gown with fitted bodice and sleeves; skirt looped up over underskirt of matching fabric, the gown trimmed with fine pleating and rosettes.

5 English gentleman: powdered wig with no side curls; knee-length coat; short double-breasted waistcoat with velvet revers and buttons; knee-breeches; silk stockings with embroidered clocks; walking stick. 6 French lady: large wig; muslin mob cap and veil with matching scarf; gown with fitted bodice and sleeves; full skirt. 7 English lady: outdoor costume: large hat with feather and ribbon trim; long curled wig; scarf with frilled edge, tied at the back; large fur muff. 8 French lady: fine muslin mob cap; full padded wig; scarf with frilled edge; gown with fitted bodice and three-quarter-length pagoda sleeves; embroidered underskirt.

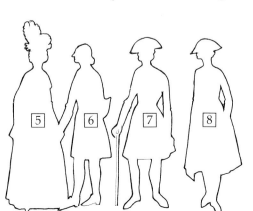

C. 1786–1788

1 French courtier *c.* 1786: large gauze mob cap; powdered wig; ankle-length gown with short sacque back, trimmed with ruffles and pleats; silk shoes and high heels. 2 French courtier *c.* 1786: wide-brimmed hat trimmed with ribbon and feathers; painted linen gown decorated with ruffles and bows; embroidered waist-belt. 3 French lady *c.* 1787: walking costume: wide-brimmed hat; wig with long ringlets; redingote with scooped neckline filled with muslin fichu; scalloped collar and tight three-quarter-length sleeves. 4 English lady *c.* 1788: hat trimmed with outsized bows; large curled and powdered wig; fine silk gown decorated with bows; matching muslin scarf and waist apron.

5 French lady *c.* 1788: travelling costume: large hat with brim turned up at one side, trimmed with feathers, ribbons and rosettes; painted, striped linen gown with wide neckline, collar and revers and deep peplum; full skirt. 6 French gentleman *c.* 1788: powdered wig with large bow and bag; fitted knee-length coat with tight sleeves, split at the back; knee-breeches; tricorn hat. 7 French gentleman *c.* 1788: bicorn hat; powdered wig; striped coat fastening from chest to waist; flared skirt; watch fob; knee-breeches; striped stockings; shoes with rosettes. 8 French gentleman *c.* 1788: bicorn hat; curled and powdered wig; stock tied into large bow; striped coat with high collar; short waistcoat; striped stockings.

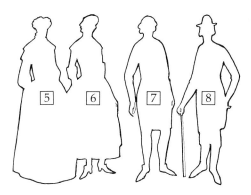

C. 1790

1 French gentleman: black beaver hat with tall crown and wide brim; stock tied into large bow; long coat buttoning from neck to waist; leather breeches; long boots; fur muff trimmed with silk bow. 2 English lady: riding habit: large hat with ribbon trim; powdered wig; stock tied into large bow; short fitted jacket with small peplum and fringed epaulettes; double-breasted waistcoat; full skirt; leather gloves. 3 French lady: large brightly coloured turban; scarf edged with lace; silk gown with fitted bodice and long tight sleeves ending in wrist frills; fine gauze apron. 4 English lady: riding habit: hat with wide brim and tall crown, trimmed with feathers; long wig; fichu; redingote with double collar and bodice, buttoned from neck to waist.

5 French lady: hair dressed over pads, with long side ringlets; fine muslin gown with wide neckline edged with lace and elbow-length sleeves; wide silk waist-sash. 6 English cook: mob cap; dress with fitted bodice and ankle-length skirt; tight sleeves with deep linen cuffs and undersleeves; matching apron and scarf. 7 French gentleman: powdered wig; fitted coat with large buttons; long fitted sleeves frilled at the wrist; knee-breeches; garters; silk stockings; flat buckled shoes. 8 American gentleman: tall beaver hat with curled brim; coat with high collar and wide revers; short waistcoat; watch fob; knee-breeches; long boots; walking stick.

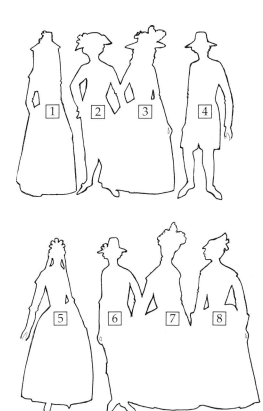

C. 1790

1 French lady: travelling costume: tall hat with wide brim, trimmed with blue, white and red ribbon and rosettes; shoulder-length veil; fichu; redingote buttoning from neck to waist; large fur muff trimmed with silk bow. 2 French gentleman: bicorn hat with blue, white and red rosette trim; stock tied into large bow; fitted coat with wide revers and contrasting collar; short striped waistcoat; striped knee-breeches; garters; silk stockings; flat pumps with bow trim. 3 French lady: travelling costume: tall hat trimmed with feathers and ribbon rosette; long curled wig; fitted jacket with wide turned-back facings; waist-sash; full skirt. 4 French gentleman: tall beaver hat; double-breasted coat with high collar; short waistcoat; two watch fobs; knee-breeches.

5 French lady: pale wig decorated with ribbon; fine muslin scarf and waist apron; wide sash; ankle-length skirt; flat pumps. 6 French gentleman: tall hat trimmed with ribbon; fitted tailcoat; double-breasted waistcoat; knee-breeches; striped stockings; long cuffed boots. 7 French lady: walking costume: hat with upturned brim and feather trim; powdered wig; double muslin scarf tied at the back; half-redingote of striped satin; satin waist-belt; silk underskirt. 8 French lady: travelling costume: small straw hat; stock tied into bow; half-redingote with double-breasted fastening.

C. 1791–1796

☐1 French lady c. 1791: walking costume: hat with feather and ribbon trim; scarf knotted in front; gown with fitted bodice and sleeves; wide waist-sash reaching to the bust. ☐2 French gentleman c. 1791: hat trimmed with blue, white and red ribbon rosette; full-length coat with high collar, striped revers and matching lining; fitted double-breasted coat; two watch fobs; knee-breeches; garters. ☐3 French lady c. 1791: wig decorated with flowers; scarf held with brooch; ruched bodice and sleeves; wide waist-sash; full skirt with geometric design on hem. ☐4 French gentleman c. 1792: beaver hat with high crown and rosette trim; fitted tailcoat; short brocade waistcoat with striped collar; leather breeches; long boots.

☐5 French gentleman c. 1792: powdered wig; striped coat; short brocade waistcoat with wide revers; watch fob; leather breeches. ☐6 French gentleman c. 1792: coat with double collar and revers, decorated and fastened with straps and buttons; short waistcoat; watch fob; leather breeches; long cuffed boots. ☐7 French lady c. 1795: hat trimmed with ribbons and feathers; muslin scarf; short jacket with long fitted sleeves; sash; full skirt. ☐8 Young French gentleman c. 1796: hair cut in untidy style; stock knotted at the throat; fitted coat with full skirt; contrasting collar and flared wrist cuffs; double-breasted waistcoat with double collar; leather breeches; striped stockings; short boots.

C. 1796–1799

☐1 French gentleman c. 1796: short cropped hair; stock tied high; coat with high collar and wide revers; short double-breasted waistcoat worn over longer single-breasted waistcoat; tight breeches to below knee; silk stockings; flat pumps. ☐2 Young French gentleman c. 1796: bicorn hat; long untidy hair; stock held with brooch; short double-breasted waistcoat; knee-length coat with fitted bodice and flared skirt; tight breeches to below knee; silk stockings; flat pumps. ☐3 Spanish noblewoman c. 1798: long dark wig; pearl necklace; fine muslin gown with ruched bodice and sleeves; wide waist-sash with long streamers at back; full skirt. ☐4 Young French gentleman c. 1798: bicorn hat with cockade; long hair; double-breasted coat with high collar and double revers; knee-breeches; ribbon garters; silk stockings; flat pumps; walking stick.

☐5 Young French lady c. 1799: short cropped hair; long earrings and pearl necklace; fine muslin gown with low scooped neckline and high waist; narrow sash under bust; long tight sleeves; narrow skirt with embroidered hem; flat silk pumps. ☐6 French gentleman c. 1799: beaver hat with shallow crown; double-breasted coat with high collar and wide lapels; waistcoat; tight breeches; long cuffed boots. ☐7 Young French lady c. 1799: walking costume: straw bonnet trimmed with violets and silk ribbon; muslin fichu; short spencer jacket; high-waisted muslin gown with long train; silk stockings with clocks; flat silk pumps. ☐8 French lady c. 1799: travelling costume: straw bonnet with tall upturned brim; high-waisted, double-breasted coat with wide collar and revers; long tight sleeves; flat silk pumps.

c. 1800-1803

English lady
c. 1800

French coachman
c. 1800

French lady
c. 1800

American maid
c. 1800

French gentleman
c. 1802

German gentleman c. 1803

Russian lady c. 1803

French lady
c. 1803

C. 1805-1810

French lady
c. 1805

English gentleman
c. 1805

French lady
c. 1808

German
seamstress
c. 1808

American gentleman
c. 1809

English lady
c. 1810

English gentleman c. 1810

American gentleman c. 1810

c. 1811-1822

English gentleman
c. 1811

English gentleman
c. 1812

English lady
c. 1812

English
gentleman
c. 1815

English lady
c. 1820

English lady c. 1816

English milkmaid c. 1820

German gentleman c. 1822

C. 1823-1828

English lady
c. 1823

German gentleman
c. 1824

English gentleman
c. 1824

American
schoolmistress
c. 1825

French lady
c. 1828

French lady
c. 1828

English gentleman c. 1825

English gentleman c. 1828

c. 1828-1832

English housemaid c. 1828

English lady c. 1828

French lady c. 1829

German lady c. 1830

German gentleman c. 1830

English lady c. 1831

English lady c. 1831

English gentleman c. 1832

C. 1832 -1840

Russian gentleman
c. 1832

English lady
c. 1834

French gentleman
c. 1835

Russian lady
c. 1832

English lady
c. 1836

English lady
c. 1836

English lady c. 1840

English gentleman c. 1840

c. 1842-1845

German gentleman
c. 1842

English lady
c. 1843

English lady
c. 1843

German gentleman
c. 1844

German gentleman
c. 1844

English lady
c. 1845

English lady c. 1845

German gentleman c. 1845

C. 1845-1850

English gentleman
c. 1845

French lady
c. 1846

English groom
c. 1848

French lady
c. 1848

Russian lady
c. 1848

American lady
c. 1848

French gentleman c. 1850

German gentleman c. 1850

C. 1850-1855

English gentleman
c. 1850

French gentleman
c. 1850

French lady
c. 1850

English gentleman
c. 1853

German gentleman
c. 1853

French lady
c. 1854

German lady c. 1854

German lady c. 1855

c. 1856-1865

German lady
c. 1856

German lady
c. 1858

American gentleman
c. 1861

English
gentleman
c. 1861

French lady
c. 1863

English lady
c. 1864

French lady
c. 1865

French middle-class woman c. 1864

c. 1865-1869

Russian lady
c. 1865

French lady
c. 1866

English carpenter
c. 1867

English
farmworker
c. 1868

Russian lady
c. 1868

English lady
c. 1869

English actress c. 1868

French lady c. 1869

c. 1871-1877

English lady
c. 1871

English
gentleman
c. 1872

German lady
c. 1873

German lady
c. 1874

German lady
c. 1875

English lady
c. 1876

English lady
c. 1877

French gentleman c. 1875

German gentleman
c. 1878

English lady
c. 1879

English lady
c. 1879

English
gentleman
c. 1880

French lady
c. 1880

German cook
c. 1881

English lady
c. 1883

American lady c. 1884

C. 1885-1890

French lady
c. 1885

French gentleman
c. 1885

Russian lady
c. 1885

French lady
c. 1886

English lady
c. 1887

American
schoolmistress
c. 1889

English lady
c. 1890

English gentleman c. 1889

c. 1891-1894

English gentleman
c. 1891

English gentleman
c. 1891

English lady
c. 1892

English butcher
c. 1893

English lady
c. 1894

English
middle-class woman
c. 1892

American lady c. 1894

French gentleman c. 1894

c. 1895-1899

German lady
c. 1895

American
gentleman
c. 1895

French lady
c. 1895

American
lady c. 1896

English gentleman
c. 1898

Russian lady
c. 1899

English shop
assistant
c. 1899

American shop assistant c. 1899

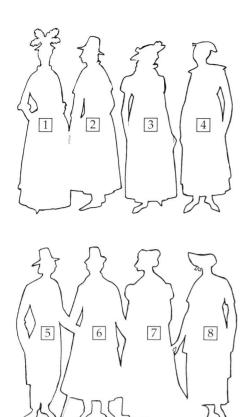

C. 1800–1803

☐ English lady *c.* 1800: travelling costume: tall-crowned hat with narrow brim and feather trim; pearl necklace; fur-trimmed coat with three-quarter-length sleeves; large fur muff. ☐ French coachman *c.* 1800: tall-crowned hat with narrow curled brim and ribbon cockade; long coat with three-tier shoulder cape; long sleeves with fur cuffs; full skirt with centre back pleat; long leather boots; leather gloves. ☐ French lady *c.* 1800: walking costume: straw hat trimmed with bows and flowers and tied under the chin with a ribbon; high-waisted gown of embroidered muslin, the neckline low with frilled edge; puff sleeves over long tight sleeves; ribbon belt; pleated hem; flat pumps. ☐ American maid *c.* 1800: cotton cap with frilled edge, point at back and ribbon and bow trim; high standing collar and circular collar of fine cotton worn over ankle-length, striped cotton dress; high-waisted, checked cotton apron; flat leather pumps.

☐ French gentleman *c.* 1802: tall-crowned hat with curled brim; double-breasted coat with tails and flap pockets; ankle-length trousers; stockings; leather pumps; walking stick. ☐ German gentleman *c.* 1803: travelling costume: tall-crowned hat; curled hair and side whiskers; long double-breasted coat with fur cuffs and matching shawl collar; long leather boots; leather gloves; walking stick. ☐ Russian lady *c.* 1803: formal court costume: hair dressed into curled fringe and back ringlets; narrow gold fillets; long drop earrings; silk satin gown with high waist and puff sleeves; sleeveless shoulder train decorated with ribbon embroidery. ☐ French lady *c.* 1803: walking costume: straw bonnet with shallow crown and deep brim, tied under the chin; fine muslin dress and matching jacket trimmed with bands of fine ribbon; parasol carried upside down; stockings; flat silk pumps with leather soles.

C. 1805–1810

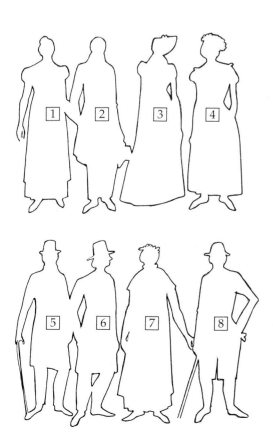

☐ French lady *c.* 1805: hair dressed into curls and ringlets; drop earrings and matching pearl necklace; fine muslin ballgown with low scooped neckline and high waist; small puff sleeves; two-tier skirt, the upper hem decorated with embroidery; long gloves; flat pumps. ☐ English gentleman *c.* 1805: shirt with high collar; stock tied into bow; coat with high collar, wide revers and flap pockets; double-breasted, striped silk waistcoat with wide revers; ankle-length trousers; flat leather pumps; leather gloves; tall-crowned hat. ☐ French lady *c.* 1808: day costume: straw bonnet with deep brim, trimmed with flowers; spotted muslin dress with high waistline and slight train; puffed oversleeves and long tight sleeves. ☐ German seamstress *c.* 1808: straw hat with feather trim; cotton dress with fitted bodice, small puff sleeves and ankle-length skirt with pleated hem; cross-over shawl tied at the back; stockings; flat pumps.

☐ American gentleman *c.* 1809: top hat; shirt with high collar; stock; tailcoat with velvet collar; waistcoat with upturned collar; ankle-length trousers; leather gloves; flat pumps worn with spats; walking cane. ☐ English gentleman *c.* 1810: top hat; shirt with high collar and frilled front; stock tied into bow; double-breasted coat with M-notch collar; ankle-length trousers; leather gloves; flat pumps with buckle trim. ☐ English lady *c.* 1810: travelling costume: small straw bonnet with ribbon trim, tied with a bow under chin; fine wool, double-breasted coat with high waist, long fitted sleeves and shawl collar arranged to give cape effect; leather gloves. ☐ American gentleman *c.* 1810: riding costume: tall-crowned hat; double-breasted coat with M-notch collar, trimmed in velvet; high-buttoned waistcoat; tight breeches; long leather boots; walking stick.

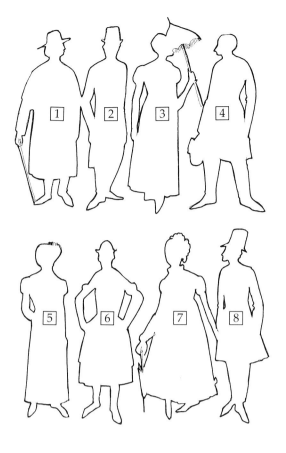

C. 1811–1822

1 English gentleman *c.* 1811: top hat; long overcoat, buttoning from high collar to hem, with elbow-length cape; long boots; leather gloves; walking stick. 2 English gentleman *c.* 1812: top hat; shirt with high collar and frilled front; cravat; coat with M-notch collar; striped silk waistcoat with shawl collar; trousers with straps under the foot; silk stockings; flat pumps with bow trim. 3 English lady *c.* 1812: walking costume: brimless bonnet covered with pleated silk and tied under the chin; short spencer jacket fastening at the front; short puffed oversleeves and long tight sleeves; spotted muslin dress with band of embroidery and pleated hem; silk stockings; flat silk pumps with leather soles; parasol. 4 English gentleman *c.* 1815: frock coat with velvet shawl collar and matching flap pockets and sleeve cuffs; ankle-length trousers; ankle-boots; wide-brimmed hat; leather gloves.

5 English lady *c.* 1816: silk-covered bonnet decorated with silk flowers and tied under the chin with ribbon bow; dress with high waist; cross-over bodice frilled at the edges; long tight sleeves and puffed oversleeves with cuffs; skirt with embroidered band on hem; embroidered and fringed shawl. 6 English milkmaid *c.* 1820: masculine, tall-crowned hat; muslin bodice with cross-over front; stays with front lacing; knee-length, two-tier skirt trimmed with ribbon; canvas spats; flat pumps. 7 English lady *c.* 1820: bonnet with pleated silk brim, the crown trimmed with feathers; high-waisted dress pleated at the wrist and hem; puff sleeves and long tight sleeves; belt of spotted ribbon and matching bow decoration on hem; flat pumps; parasol. 8 German gentleman *c.* 1822: tall-crowned top hat; checked wool frock coat with velvet collar and flared skirt; high-buttoned waistcoat; checked trousers; leather gloves; leather ankle-boots.

C. 1823–1828

1 English lady *c.* 1823: silk-lined straw bonnet with silk flower and ribbon trim, tied under the chin in a bow; lace collar; short spencer jacket of embroidered silk with puffed sleeves over long tight sleeves; ankle-length skirt; short gloves; embroidered bag; flat pumps. 2 German gentleman *c.* 1824: top hat; checked wool coat with contrasting M-notch collar and revers; high-buttoned waistcoat; trousers with side pockets, narrow legs and straps under the foot; ankle-boots. 3 English gentleman *c.* 1824: formal evening wear: shirt with high collar; silk cravat; swallowtail coat; silk waistcoat with shawl collar; knee-length velvet breeches; silk stockings; flat pumps with silver buckles. 4 American schoolmistress *c.* 1825: wool dress with fitted bodice, large puffed sleeves and full skirt; cotton apron with patch pockets.

5 English gentleman *c.* 1825: top hat; checked wool coat and elbow-length cape with long collar, the edges top-stitched; leather gloves; checked wool trousers; boots; walking stick. 6 English gentleman *c.* 1828: tall top hat; shirt with high collar; silk cravat; double-breasted wool coat with velvet collar; checked wool trousers; leather boots with shiny toe caps. 7 French lady *c.* 1828: large beret trimmed with rosette and feathers; high-waisted ballgown with large puffed sleeves; full skirt supported by stiff petticoats, the hem trimmed with ruched ribbon, bows and silk flowers; long gloves; silk pumps. 8 French lady *c.* 1828: large brimmed hat lined with pleated silk, the crown trimmed with feathers; patterned dress and matching silk coat with fine silk fringe; large puffed sleeves; high waist-belt; small embroidered muff.

C. 1828–1832

[1] English housemaid *c.* 1828: cotton mob cap; spotted cotton neck scarf; striped cotton shift with high waist and wide short sleeves; long cotton apron; leather ankle-boots. [2] English lady *c.* 1828: bonnet with high brim lined with silk, the crown trimmed with feathers; wide lace collar; long coat with small shoulder cape; large puffed sleeves and tight undersleeves; embroidered belt; full skirt worn over petticoats, trimmed with ribbons and lace; fur muff; silk stockings; flat pumps. [3] French lady *c.* 1829: bonnet with very wide brim and embroidered lining, the crown trimmed with silk flowers and looped ribbons; frilled collar; neck scarf; dress with high waist; full skirt worn over petticoats; wide sleeves topped with frilled epaulettes; flat pumps with ribbon ties. [4] German lady *c.* 1830: hair dressed into a bun and false side ringlets; drop earrings; ballgown with off-the-shoulder neckline; long fitted sleeves and puffed sleeves trimmed with lace to match the cuffs.

[5] German gentleman *c.* 1830: top hat; shirt with high collar; cravat; ankle-length overcoat, buttoning to hem, with velvet collar and narrow cuffs; double-breasted waistcoat and narrow trousers in matching checked wool; ankle-boots. [6] English lady *c.* 1831: simply dressed hair decorated with loops of false hair and pearls; drop earrings and pearl necklace; ballgown with high waist and off-the-shoulder neckline; large puffed sleeves with silk flower trim; matching garlands on either side of open skirt. [7] English lady *c.* 1831: hair dressed with false ringlets and silk flowers; ballgown with wide cape collar embroidered with flowers to match the skirt; long gloves; flat pumps. [8] English gentleman *c.* 1832: top hat; double-breasted coat with brass buttons and full skirt; leather gloves; trousers with straps under the foot; walking stick.

C. 1832–1840

[1] Russian lady *c.* 1832: bonnet with large brim, the crown trimmed with feathers, looped ribbon and lace veil; neck ruff; ankle-length day dress with high waist-belt and large puffed sleeves; richly embroidered shawl collar and front skirt panel with matching muff; pleated underbodice; fine leather button boots. [2] Russian gentleman *c.* 1832: tall top hat; high wing collar; silk cravat; double-breasted, ankle-length coat lined and trimmed in fur; narrow trousers; boots; walking stick. [3] English lady *c.* 1834: hair dressed with stiffened loops of false hair and silk flowers; drop earrings and matching pearl necklace; evening gown of embroidered silk; off-the-shoulder neckline with pleated edge; large puffed sleeves with frilled epaulettes; embroidered belt; stiff bodice worn over corset; full skirt. [4] French gentleman *c.* 1835: riding costume: top hat; high cravat worn over wing collar; fitted coat with high collar, revers and full skirt; waistcoat with shawl collar; leather gloves; tight breeches; high leather boots.

[5] English lady *c.* 1836: bonnet lined with pleated silk and trimmed with feathers and ribbons; elbow-length, tiered shoulder cape with braid trimming; striped silk dress with large puffed oversleeves; high waist-belt; full skirt supported over stiffened petticoats; small fur muff. [6] English lady *c.* 1836: bonnet with silk ribbon trim; dress with tight bodice worn over corset; large puffed sleeves with frilled epaulettes; wide skirt; fine cashmere shawl; silk pumps. [7] English lady *c.* 1840: hair decorated with ribbons and silk flowers; evening gown with off-the-shoulder neckline and fitted bodice; tiered skirt with scalloped edge; long gloves; folding fan. [8] English gentleman *c.* 1840: evening dress: high wing collar; silk cravat; swallowtail coat with silk-faced collar and revers; waistcoat with shawl collar; narrow trousers with side pockets and straps under the foot; flat pumps.

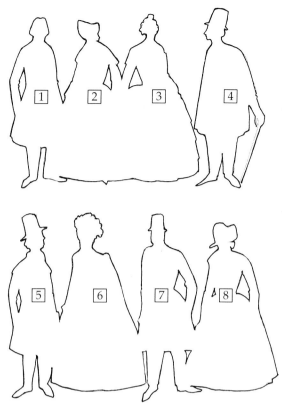

C. 1842–1845

1 German gentleman c. 1842: high collared shirt; silk cravat tied in bow; velvet jacket with sloping hip pockets and full skirt; contrasting collar and cuffs; narrow trousers; leather ankle-boots. 2 English lady c. 1843: bonnet covered with pleated silk and trimmed with lace frill at back; silk taffeta dress with lace collar, boned bodice, corset and flared sleeves; tiered skirt worn over petticoats and crinoline and trimmed with velvet ribbon and fine fringe. 3 English lady c. 1843: evening gown: silk dress woven with flowers; off-the-shoulder neckline; deep lace-edged collar; matching hem of tiered skirt and flared sleeves; false undersleeves. 4 German gentleman c. 1844: tall top hat; shirt with high collar; silk cravat tied in bow; knee-length tweed coat with high fastening and flap pockets; narrow trousers made of striped fabric; leather gloves and boots.

5 German gentleman c. 1844: tall top hat; shirt with high stiff collar; silk cravat; stock pin; double-breasted overcoat with small shoulder cape, fur collar and cuffs; striped wool trousers with straps under the foot. 6 English lady c. 1845: bonnet covered with silk and trimmed with feathers; checked wool pelisse buttoning from the neck to the waist; fur collar and trimming. 7 German gentleman c. 1845: top hat; double-breasted coat fastening from the chest to the waist; narrow shawl collar; slanting flap pockets; narrow cuffs; leather gloves; walking stick. 8 English lady c. 1845: straw bonnet trimmed with ribbon; fitted velvet jacket, buttoning from high neckline to the waist, with decorative braids and buttons; tight sleeves with narrow epaulettes; lace detail at wrist to match lace collar; striped silk skirt.

C. 1845–1850

1 English gentleman c. 1845: tall top hat; shirt with high stiff collar; silk cravat; knee-length fitted coat with wide collar and revers; waistcoat with high button fastening and two pockets; trousers with side pockets; leather boots. 2 French lady c. 1846: bonnet covered with silk and trimmed with posey of flowers and lace frill at back; fitted jacket buttoning from high neck to waist; fur collar and trimming; narrow peplum; full skirt worn over petticoats and crinoline; fur muff. 3 English groom c. 1848: top hat; short coat in striped tweed with flared skirt and plain collar; striped waistcoat with shawl collar; tight breeches buttoning at the knee; long leather gaiters; short leather boots. 4 French lady c. 1848: small bonnet trimmed with embroidered ribbon, posey of flowers and lace frill; large cashmere shawl with wide decorative border and fringe and tassel edges; tiered skirt; fur muff; leather gloves.

5 Russian lady c. 1848: hair tied back with silk ribbons; dress with boned bodice over corset; silk ribbon waist-belt; tiered lace skirt and matching sleeve frills. 6 American lady c. 1848: bonnet trimmed with ribbon, flowers and lace frill; silk taffeta dress and pelisse trimmed with bands of fine net ribbon; false undersleeves; full skirt supported over stiff petticoats and crinoline; leather gloves. 7 French gentleman c. 1850: evening suit: silk top hat; cape with collar and revers, lined in brightly coloured silk; shirt with high collar and frilled front; narrow bow tie; fitted waistcoat; swallowtail coat and matching trousers; gloves; fine leather boots; walking stick. 8 German gentleman c. 1850: top hat; high shirt collar; silk bow tie; short double-breasted coat with fur collar and large horn buttons, the wrist and hem inset with band of plain fabric; narrow trousers; leather gloves and boots.

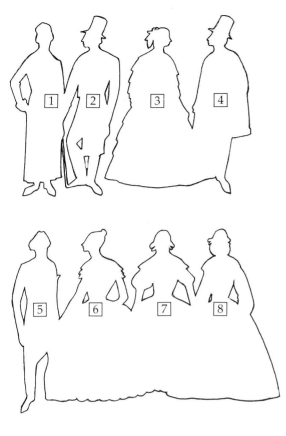

C. 1850–1855

1. English gentleman c. 1850: small brimless hat with embroidered decoration and long tassel; dressing gown with wrapover front; cord tie fastening; large quilted shawl collar; matching cuffs and patch pockets; leather mules. 2. French gentleman c. 1850: top hat; high shirt collar; silk bow tie; double-breasted coat with braided edges, cut away to reveal waistcoat; checked wool trousers; leather gloves and boots; walking stick. 3. French lady c. 1850: hair tied back with ribbons and lace scarf; lace collar; brooch; silk taffeta day dress with high round neckline, boned bodice and corset; sleeves and full skirt cut in tiers and trimmed with fine ribbon trim; false undersleeves. 4. English gentleman c. 1853: top hat; high shirt collar; patterned cravat; short overcoat with fur collar, cuffs, trimming and lining, fastened in the front with cord and horn buttons; checked wool trousers.

5. German gentleman c. 1853: town riding costume: high shirt collar; silk cravat; double-breasted swallowtail coat with slanting pockets, the breast pocket containing silk handkerchief; narrow trousers; boots worn with spurs. 6. German lady c. 1854: evening gown with off-the-shoulder neckline, lace collar, boned bodice and corset; tiered lace skirt worn over crinoline and petticoats; short gloves. 7. French lady c. 1854: evening gown with off-the-shoulder neckline and double collar; small puffed sleeves; boned bodice and corset; crinoline skirt trimmed with wide bands of lace. 8. German lady c. 1855: hair held in a net; lace collar and brooch; striped silk day dress with boned bodice, buttoning from the neck to the waist; corset; sleeves trimmed with pleated ruffles to match skirt, crinoline and petticoats.

C. 1856–1865

1. German lady c. 1856: small bonnet with pleated edge and lace frill at back; lace collar; velvet jacket with fitted bodice; decorative braid and button fastening; deep peplum; leather gloves; fur muff; full skirt over crinoline. 2. German lady c. 1858: hair dressed away from face; back of head covered with lace veil; pearl necklace; pearl and cameo bracelet; silk taffeta ballgown woven with pattern of flowers; off-the-shoulder neckline edged in plain silk and two rows of lace; matching lace sleeves; boned bodice; corset; full skirt over crinoline, trimmed with ribbons and bows; folding fan. 3. American gentleman c. 1861: hard felt derby; curled moustache; shirt with turned-down collar; cravat; jacket with single button fastening, narrow collar, revers and patch pockets; checked wool trousers; gloves; walking stick. 4. English gentleman c. 1861: country wear: hard felt bowler; curled moustache; shirt with turned-down collar; cravat; double-breasted waistcoat with collar and revers; tweed jacket with patch pockets; knickerbockers gathered into band at the knee; leather gaiters and short boots.

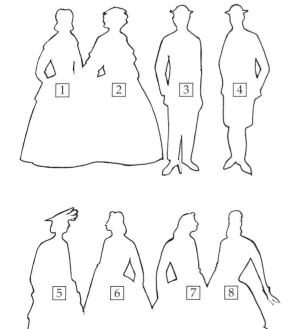

5. French lady c. 1863: walking costume: hat with wide brim and small crown, trimmed with feathers; short, flared wool coat trimmed with braid and satin ribbon; three-quarter-length sleeves with deep cuffs; wide revers; deep pocket. 6. English lady c. 1864: striped cotton shirt; turned-down collar with embroidered motif; matching sleeve cuffs; wide belt with buckle; plain skirt. 7. French middle-class woman c. 1864: hair dressed into net at the back and curled fringe at the front; short close-fitting jacket; day dress with high neckline, boned bodice and corset; flared sleeves; false undersleeves; skirt with pleated hem. 8. French lady c. 1865: silk day dress trimmed with fine pleating at the neck, shoulder, wrist and hem; skirt tied back with satin ribbon bows.

C. 1865–1869

[1] Russian lady c. 1865: flat lace collar; silk day dress with high round neckline; boned bodice; front opening; corset; fringe and button trimming on bodice and sleeve cuffs; tiered skirt decorated with bands of embroidery. [2] French lady c. 1866: pearl necklace and matching drop earrings; ballgown with off-the-shoulder neckline; small puff sleeves; raised waistline emphasized by belt with round buckle; deep peplum dips to each side of skirt, the hems decorated with bands of ribbon; long gloves. [3] English carpenter c. 1867: folded paper hat; neck scarf; waistcoat; jacket with patch pockets; waist apron; trousers; ankle-boots. [4] English farmworker c. 1868: straw hat with large crown and wide brim; neck scarf; knee-length, coarse linen smock; large flat collar, the edges embroidered with simple stitches to match high yoke seam, sleeve head and cuff; front-lacing long boots.

[5] Russian lady c. 1868: town dress: tiny bonnet with upturned brim, trimmed with lace frill and silk flowers, and tied under the chin; silk parasol with lace edging; striped silk taffeta gown with raised waistline; boned bodice; corset; front of skirt, hem of deep peplum and sleeve cuff trimmed with bands and buttons of self fabric. [6] English actress c. 1868: stage costume: small hat decorated with feathers and rosette; dress with boned bodice and corset; skirt looped up at each side and trimmed with pleating and ribbon; ankle-length underskirt with deep frill at hem; high button boots with louis heels. [7] English lady c. 1869: tiny straw hat trimmed with silk flower petals; high-necked lace jacket with tiny collar, flared sleeves and deep peplum; ribbon belt. [8] French lady c. 1869: riding costume: small hat with transparent veil at the back; shirt with high collar, cravat and pin; fitted velvet jacket with raised waist; belt; fringed peplum and skirt hem; gauntlets.

C. 1871–1877

[1] English lady c. 1871: small straw hat trimmed with flowers and ribbon; large plait of hair; embroidered dress, trimmed with flat ribbon and pleated silk, with boned bodice and looped-up skirt forming bustle; plain silk skirt. [2] English gentleman c. 1872: top hat; stiff shirt collar; cravat; fur-lined and -trimmed cashmere overcoat; leather gloves; checked wool trousers. [3] German lady c. 1873: small pill-box hat with posey of flowers, tied under the chin; dress trimmed with embroidered ribbon, pleating and ribbon braid; fitted boned bodice; corset; long tight sleeves; skirt tied back; bustle; deep peplum; floating panels. [4] German lady c. 1874: drop earrings; silk day dress; boned bodice cut with deep peplum and pleated ribbon trim; three rows of decorative buttons from high round neckline to waist; brooch in middle of collar.

[5] French gentleman c. 1875: shirt with turned-down collar; necktie with large knot; swallowtail coat with three buttons; waistcoat; narrow trousers. [6] German lady c. 1875: day dress; boned bodice extended to low hip; corset; front panel, stand collar and sleeve cuffs made of fine silk velvet; narrow skirt draped and trimmed with frills, lace, ribbons and pleating. [7] English lady c. 1876: small bonnet trimmed with silk flowers and ribbons; dress with buttons from high neckline to hem; boned bodice fitted over hips; corset; tiny patch pockets; tiered underskirt of fine pleated silk. [8] English lady c. 1877: calling costume: hat trimmed with large feathers; gown with long boned bodice fitted over hips; pleated collar; corset; long tight sleeves with deep cuff; narrow skirt tied at the back to form train and decorated with ribbon, braid, tassels and fringing.

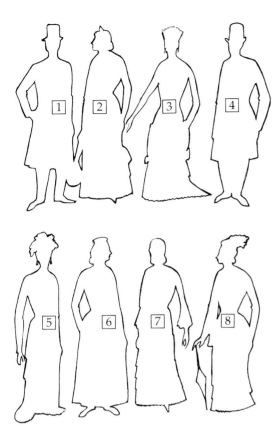

C. 1878–1884

1 German gentleman c. 1878: top hat; stiff shirt collar and cuffs; cravat with pin; waistcoat with high fastening; double-breasted frock coat with silk facing on collar, revers and sleeve cuffs, the pockets cut into side seams; narrow trousers. 2 English lady c. 1879: tennis costume: pleated headband; rib at high round neck and wrist; long fitted jersey extending over hips; long tight sleeves; pleated skirt; canvas shoes. 3 English lady c. 1879: small, stiffened felt hat with flower and ribbon trim; necklace and matching earrings; dress with boned bodice to low hip; long collar and revers; tight sleeves; draped overskirt; tiered underskirt of pleated silk forming train. 4 English gentleman c. 1880: top hat; large moustache, beard and side whiskers; shirt with stiff collar and cuffs; bow tie; double-breasted, checked wool frock coat; collar, revers, flap pockets and cuffs bound with silk braid; narrow checked trousers; boots.

5 French lady c. 1880: small hat trimmed with feathers; long fitted jacket extended to low hip; decorative braid on collar, revers, cuffs of narrow sleeves, hipline and overskirt; leather gloves; small cloth bag with cord handle, trimmed with a tassel. 6 German cook c. 1881: small mob cap; dress with fitted bodice and ankle-length skirt; long cotton bib apron; matching collar and cuffs; leather boots.
7 English lady c. 1883: silk day dress with stand collar and lace frill at neck; fall of lace from the neck to the waist; three-quarter-length sleeves with lace frills; long boned bodice; corset; narrow skirt with drapery and pleats. 8 American lady c. 1884: small hat with upturned brim and feather trim; scarf tucked into waistcoat; fitted jacket with collar and revers; narrow skirt with drapery and pleats; leather gloves; umbrella.

C. 1885–1890

1 French lady c. 1885: bathing costume: large cap gathered on to band; bathing dress trimmed with braid and pleating; wide collar with bow trim; fitted bodice; buttons from the neck to the waist; short sleeves; knee-length underdrawers; flat pumps with ribbon ties. 2 French gentleman c. 1885: bathing costume: knitted top and drawers cut in one piece; button opening from the neck to the waist; flat pumps with ribbon straps. 3 Russian lady c. 1885: embroidered silk day dress, the low neckline edged with frilled lace; matching undercuff of three-quarter-length sleeves and matching lace hip seam; long boned bodice; corset; skirt with scalloped hem forming long train. 4 French lady c. 1886: hat with tall crown and upturned brim, trimmed with looped ribbon and flowers; brocade dress with deep plunge neckline; infill of plain silk with high stand collar; boned bodice; corset; tight sleeves; skirt tied at the back to form bustle; pleated hem.

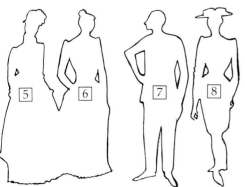

5 English lady c. 1887: hat with tall crown, narrow brim and feather trim; wool coat with fitted bodice, small peplum and full skirt; high fur collar; matching cuffs, buttons and trimming. 6 American schoolmistress c. 1889: striped cotton dress buttoning down the front in sets of two; stand collar; boned bodice extended over hips; corset; narrow sleeves; small cuffs; narrow skirt; draped apron of checked cotton; matching inset band on hem. 7 English gentleman c. 1889: shirt with high stiff collar and cuffs; bow tie; waistcoat with shawl collar, two pockets, watch and chain; matching jacket and trousers; cotton gloves. 8 English lady c. 1890: cycling costume: straw hat with shallow crown and stiff brim; shirt with turned-down collar; knitted jersey; Norfolk jacket with box pleats, collar and revers, and button fastening; self-fabric waist-belt; knickerbockers gathered at the knee; long spats.

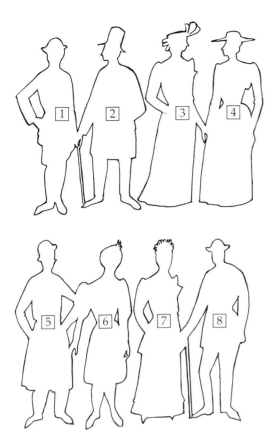

C. 1891–1894

1 English gentleman *c.* 1891: country wear: bowler hat; moustache; shirt with high stand collar; cravat and stock pin; Norfolk jacket with box pleats, narrow collar and revers, and high button fastening; self-fabric belt and patch pockets; knickerbockers gathered into wide band at the knee; knitted stockings; lace-up boots. 2 English gentleman *c.* 1891: top hat; knee-length coat with shoulder cape, concealed fastening and patch pockets; leather gloves; walking stick. 3 English lady *c.* 1892: straw hat with shallow crown and wide stiff brim, trimmed with wired ribbons; tailored jacket with wide collar and revers, the long tight sleeves gathered at the head; tailored skirt cut in flared panels; blouse with turned-down collar, buttons down the front and frilled edge. 4 English middle-class woman *c.* 1892: shallow crowned straw boater with wide stiff brim and ribbon trim; blouse with stand collar and gathered bodice; short bolero jacket with wide collar and braid trim; skirt gathered at the waist, the hem decorated with braid; wide cummerbund.

5 English butcher *c.* 1893: bowler hat; shirt with wing collar; necktie; knee-length white cotton coat, collar and revers with high button fastening; plain waist apron; striped waist apron; striped trousers. 6 American lady *c.* 1894: cycling costume: beret trimmed with brooch and feather; waist-length fitted jacket with leg-of-mutton sleeves; bloomers gathered at the knee; long spats; boots. 7 English lady *c.* 1894: blouse with stand collar; bow tie; three-piece tailored outfit, the jacket with wide collar, revers and leg-of-mutton sleeves; fitted waistcoat; skirt cut in panels. 8 French gentleman *c.* 1894: bowler hat; two-piece suit in matching checked wool, the jacket with high button fastening and flap pockets; narrow trousers.

C. 1895–1899

1 German lady *c.* 1895: riding habit: transparent veil attached to top hat; masculine shirt and cravat; tailored coat with velvet collar, revers and high button fastening; tight red waistcoat; long skirt with train; wool petticoat. 2 American gentleman *c.* 1895: cycling outfit: derby; shirt with wing collar; necktie with large knot; waistcoat; double-breasted jacket with three welt pockets; knickerbockers gathered at the knee; knitted socks; leather brogues. 3 French lady *c.* 1895: bathing costume: gathered cap trimmed with large bow; broad striped, knitted bathing dress; wide lace neckline; short skirt; waist-belt; knee-length drawers with lace trim; pumps with ribbon laces. 4 American lady *c.* 1896: bathing costume: knotted head scarf; bathing dress with puffed sleeves; large collar, hem of full skirt and drawers trimmed with lace; pumps with ribbon laces.

5 English gentleman *c.* 1898: bowler hat; overcoat with velvet collar and concealed fastening; raglan sleeves with narrow cuffs; hip pockets; striped trousers; walking stick. 6 Russian lady *c.* 1899: small hat covered with petals; shoulder cape embroidered with ribbon and trimmed with fur; long fitted coat with scalloped edges and small train; striped insert with wide collar; lace-trimmed parasol. 7 English shop assistant *c.* 1899: striped cotton blouse with stand collar, gathered at the waist; puff sleeves over long fitted sleeves; flared skirt. 8 American shop assistant *c.* 1899: straw boater; fitted blouse opening down the front; leg-of-mutton sleeves; stock in matching fabric; flared skirt; umbrella; soft leather boots.

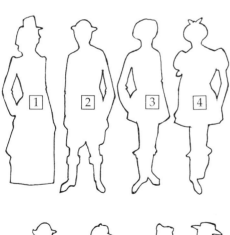

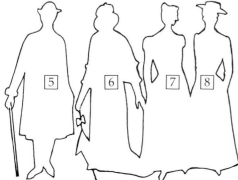

c. 1900-1903

French lady
c. 1900

German gentleman
c. 1900

German gentleman
c. 1901

English lady
c. 1901

French lady
c. 1902

German lady
c. 1902

French lady
c. 1903

German gentleman c. 1903

c. 1904-1906

Frenchwoman c. 1904

English gentleman c. 1904

English nurse c. 1905

English nurse c. 1905

Englishman c. 1905

French lady c. 1906

American lady c. 1905

English gentleman c. 1906

C. 1907-1910

English lady
c. 1907

French lady
c. 1907

German lady
c. 1908

American woman
c. 1908

English lady
c. 1909

French lady
c. 1910

American businessman c. 1909

American gentleman c. 1909

American man c. 1910

c. 1910-1913

German lady
c. 1910

French lady
c. 1910

Englishwoman
c. 1910

English lady
c. 1911

French lady
c. 1912

English lady
c. 1911

English lady c. 1911

German lady c. 1913

c. 1914-1917

English gentleman
c. 1914

English nurse
c. 1914

French lady
c. 1914

German
gentleman
c. 1915

American lady
c. 1916

American lady
c. 1916

American man c. 1916

English lady c. 1917

Englishman
c. 1917

Frenchwoman
c. 1917

American woman
c. 1918

Frenchwoman
c. 1918

Frenchwoman
c. 1919

Frenchman
c. 1919

American woman
c. 1920

Englishman c. 1920

c. 1920-1923

American man
c. 1920

American woman
c. 1920

Englishwoman
c. 1921

American woman
c. 1921

American woman
c. 1921

American waitress
c. 1923

German woman
c. 1923

Englishman c. 1922

c. 1924-1926

Frenchwoman
c. 1924

American woman
c. 1924

American woman
c. 1924

American man
c. 1925

Englishman
c. 1925

Frenchwoman
c. 1926

Frenchwoman c. 1925

German woman c. 1926

C. 1927-1930

German woman
c. 1927

American man
c. 1927

Frenchwoman
c. 1928

American man
c. 1928

Englishwoman
c. 1929

Frenchwoman
c. 1929

Frenchwoman c. 1928

Englishwoman c. 1930

American man
c. 1930

Englishman
c. 1930

American woman
c. 1930

English maid
c. 1930

American woman
c. 1931

Englishwoman c. 1932

Frenchwoman c. 1931

Frenchwoman c. 1932

c. 1933-1936

Englishman c. 1933

American woman
c. 1933

American man
c. 1934

Englishwoman
c. 1934

Frenchwoman
c. 1934

Frenchman
c. 1935

Frenchwoman
c. 1935

Englishwoman c. 1936

c. 1936-1940

American woman
c. 1936

Frenchwoman
c. 1937

Englishwoman
c. 1938

Englishwoman
c. 1938

Frenchwoman
c. 1939

American woman
c. 1940

Englishwoman c. 1939

Englishwoman c. 1940

c. 1940-1943

Englishwoman c. 1940

Englishwoman c. 1940

Englishman c. 1941

Englishwoman c. 1942

American woman c. 1942

American woman c. 1942

Englishman c. 1943

American woman c. 1943

c. 1944-1947

American woman c. 1944

Englishwoman
c. 1944

Englishman
c. 1945

American woman
c. 1946

Englishwoman
c. 1946

Englishman
c. 1947

American man c. 1946

Frenchwoman c. 1947

c. 1947-1950

Frenchwoman
c. 1947

American man
c. 1948

Englishwoman
c. 1948

American man
c. 1949

Englishwoman
c. 1949

American man
c. 1949

Frenchman c. 1950

American woman c. 1950

Englishman
c. 1950

American woman
c. 1950

Englishman
c. 1951

Frenchwoman
c. 1951

Frenchwoman
c. 1952

Englishwoman
c. 1953

American woman c. 1952

Frenchwoman c. 1953

c. 1953-1956

Englishwoman
c. 1953

Englishman
c. 1954

Frenchwoman
c. 1954

Englishwoman
c. 1954

Englishwoman
c. 1955

Frenchwoman
c. 1955

Englishman c. 1956

Englishwoman c. 1956

c. 1956-1959

American woman
c. 1956

American woman
c. 1956

American woman
c. 1957

Englishman
c. 1957

Frenchwoman
c. 1958

Frenchwoman
c. 1959

Frenchwoman
c. 1958

Englishwoman c. 1958

Frenchwoman c. 1959

C. 1960-1964

American woman c. 1960

Englishwoman
c. 1960

Englishwoman
c. 1961

Englishwoman
c. 1961

Englishwoman
c. 1963

American woman
c. 1964

Frenchwoman c. 1964

Englishwoman c. 1964

Englishwoman
c. 1965

Italian man
c. 1966

Frenchwoman
c. 1966

Englishwoman
c. 1966

Italian man
c. 1967

Frenchwoman
c. 1967

Englishwoman c. 1967

Italian man c. 1967

c. 1967-1969

Frenchman
c. 1967

American woman
c. 1968

Frenchwoman c. 1968

Frenchwoman
c. 1968

Frenchwoman
c. 1968

Englishwoman
c. 1969

American woman c. 1969   Englishwoman c. 1969

c. 1970-1972

Frenchman
c. 1970

Italian woman
c. 1970

Frenchwoman
c. 1970

American woman
c. 1970

American woman
c. 1971

Englishwoman c. 1971

Frenchman c. 1972

American woman
c. 1972

c. 1973-1976

Englishman
c. 1973

Englishwoman
c. 1973

American man
c. 1974

American
woman
c. 1974

Italian man
c. 1975

Englishwoman
c. 1976

American woman c. 1975

Frenchwoman c. 1976

Italian woman
c. 1977

Italian man
c. 1977

Italian man
c. 1978

Englishwoman
c. 1978

Englishwoman
c. 1979

Italian man
c. 1980

Englishwoman c. 1980

Italian woman c. 1980

C. 1900–1903

1 French lady *c.* 1900: travelling costume: small fur- and feather-trimmed hat; double-breasted jacket with leg-of-mutton sleeves, fur collar and cuffs; matching fur muff; leather gloves. 2 German gentleman *c.* 1900: knee-length coat with wide collar, revers and cape sleeves; shirt with stiff collar; narrow bow tie; waistcoat with shawl collar; long jacket; narrow trousers; top hat; leather gloves. 3 German gentleman *c.* 1901: trilby; shirt with wing collar; large bow tie; long jacket with braided edges, four flap pockets and single breast pocket; matching trousers; leather gloves and boots; walking stick. 4 English lady *c.* 1901: hair parted in the centre and dressed over pads; wool day dress with lace-edged collar and bertha; matching lace cuffs on bishop sleeves; fitted and boned bodice worn over corset; velvet belt; flared skirt with tucks on hem and train.

5 French lady *c.* 1902: walking costume: straw boater; blouse with stand collar; front opening; bow decoration; jacket with long tight sleeves; strap and button decoration on wrist with matching detail on bodice and flared skirt; leather belt with metal buckle; leather gloves; umbrella. 6 German lady *c.* 1902: calling costume: large hat trimmed with ribbons, bows and pleated silk; blouse with stand collar and lace jabot; jacket with braid decoration on wrist to match detail on jacket and skirt; flared skirt with train; leather gloves; long umbrella. 7 French lady *c.* 1903: calling costume: straw boater trimmed with silk roses; cotton dress covered with lace; stand collar; short pleated overbodice; elbow-length fitted sleeves with wide frill; flared skirt, the hem decorated with rows of frills; lace mittens. 8 German gentleman *c.* 1903: country costume: large tweed cap; silk cravat; waistcoat; fine tweed Norfolk jacket with yoke seam, sewn pleats, large patch pockets and buttoned belt; gathered knee-breeches; long wool socks; leather gloves; leather ankle-boots.

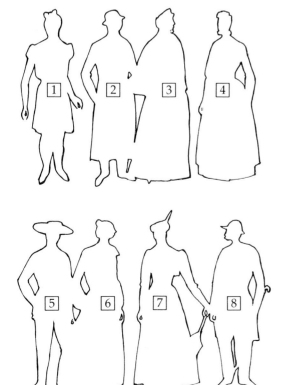

C. 1904–1906

1 Frenchwoman *c.* 1904: bathing costume: turban with large bow; knee-length, cotton bathing dress with puff sleeves; belt; contrasting colour bindings, pipings, buttons and frills; cotton stockings; flat pumps with ribbon ties. 2 English gentleman *c.* 1904: bowler hat; long double-breasted coat with velvet collar, wide revers and flap pockets; leather gloves; button boots; walking stick. 3 English nurse *c.* 1905: outdoor uniform: small pleated cap tied under chin; stiff felt cape with stand collar, the seams and edges top-stitched; dress buttoning down the front from neck to hem; leather gloves and boots. 4 English nurse *c.* 1905: indoor uniform: frilled cap with ribbon ties under chin; detachable starched collar and cuffs; dress with fitted sleeves and floor-length skirt; cotton bib apron with wide waistband, gathered skirt and large patch pockets.

5 Englishman *c.* 1905: straw boater; short hair and curled moustache; shirt and necktie; linen suit, the jacket with high button fastening, breast pocket and flap pockets, the trousers narrow; leather shoes. 6 American lady *c.* 1905: hair dressed over pads into high bun; pearl earrings and matching necklace; afternoon dress with wide neckline edged with lace; matching short oversleeves; undersleeves of pleated silk chiffon, gathered into deep cuffs; fitted bodice worn over corset; narrow belt; flared skirt decorated at hem with bows and pleated chiffon. 7 French lady *c.* 1906: small hat trimmed with feather; blouse with stand collar, trimmed with a bow and covered buttons; bolero jacket with leg-of-mutton sleeves, pleated bodice and braid trimming; skirt cut in flared panels from high waist and ending in pleats; leather gloves; umbrella. 8 English gentleman *c.* 1906: bowler hat; shirt with wing collar; necktie; waistcoat; knee-length coat with flap pockets; trousers; leather shoes worn with spats; leather gloves; walking stick.

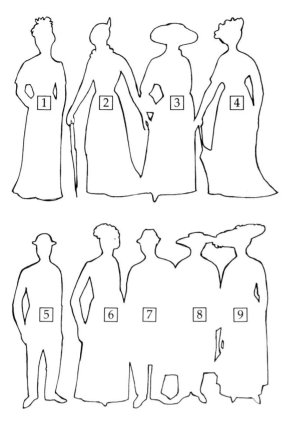

C. 1907–1910

1 English lady c. 1907: large straw hat with upturned brim and feather trim; lace blouse with stand collar; bolero jacket with braid and button trim; fitted dress with long tight sleeves, the flared skirt with train; fur muff. 2 French lady c. 1907: fur hat trimmed with brooch and feather; blouse with stand collar; detachable fur collar with brooch and bow trim; long jacket ending in point at front and buttoning from neck to waist; flared skirt cut in panels and ending in pleats; leather gloves; umbrella. 3 German lady c. 1908: hat with wide brim and large crown, draped with fabric; pleated blouse with stand collar and button fastening, the sleeves gathered at elbow; bow trim at wrist to match bow on collar; double-breasted waistcoat; sleeveless bolero with fur trim; pleated skirt. 4 American woman c. 1908: large hat with upturned brim and silk flower and bow trim; blouse with stand collar; silk dress with low square neckline, pleated bodice and sleeves; high waist-sash; skirt with train; long gloves.

5 American businessman c. 1909: derby; short hair; moustache; shirt with round collar; necktie; striped wool suit, the jacket with high button fastening and piped pockets; narrow trousers; leather shoes. 6 English lady c. 1909: hat trimmed with brooch and feather; blouse with stand collar and pleated bodice; tailored jacket with edge-to-edge fastening and fitted sleeves with deep cuffs; flared skirt with centre box pleat; umbrella. 7 American gentleman c. 1909: homburg; knee-length coat with concealed fastening, breast pocket and three flap pockets; narrow trousers; leather shoes with spats. 8 American man c. 1910: straw boater; long rainproof coat with high concealed fastening, deep collar and welt pockets; narrow trousers; leather shoes. 9 French lady c. 1910: hat with wide brim and feather trim; infill of lace with stand collar; low neckline, short sleeves, edges of overskirt, all trimmed with embroidered and beaded braid; long lace mittens; velvet handbag.

C. 1910–1913

1 German lady c. 1910: straw hat trimmed with silk roses; dress with buttons from neck to hem; low neckline infilled with lace to match three-quarter-length sleeves; high waist-belt; leather gloves and shoes; velvet bag with chain handle. 2 French lady c. 1910: felt hat with wide crown and upturned brim; blouse with stand collar and horizontal tucks; short, double-breasted half jacket with fur collar and top-stitched seams; long jacket; ankle-length skirt with side split. 3 Englishwoman c. 1910: hat with deep upturned brim; waterproof cotton coat with raglan sleeves and large patch and flap pockets; leather gloves and boots. 4 English lady c. 1911: spotted cotton dress, the wide collar edged with embroidered braid to match sleeve cuffs, hem of peplum and apron front; high waist-belt trimmed with rosette; ankle-length skirt with side split; leather shoes with high heels and instep straps.

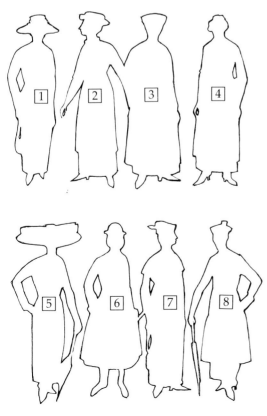

5 English lady c. 1911: hat with very wide brim, trimmed with outsized bow; lace blouse with stand collar; tailored wool suit; strap and button decoration on double-breasted jacket, sleeve hem and side pleats of narrow skirt; leather gloves and boots; umbrella. 6 English lady c. 1911: riding costume: bowler hat; hair worn in net snood; stock with decorative pin; long tailored jacket with single-breasted fastening from revers to waist and flared skirt; leather gauntlets; long boots. 7 French lady c. 1912: straw hat with feather trim; lace blouse with stand collar and long tight sleeves; dress with large cap sleeves; leather belt under bust; narrow skirt with asymmetric overskirt; velvet bag with long handle; leather shoes with buckle. 8 German lady c. 1913: straw hat with wide upturned brim and feather trim; dress with dolman sleeves, deep cotton cuffs and matching collar; gathered overskirt; ankle-length narrow skirt; cotton gloves; umbrella; button boots.

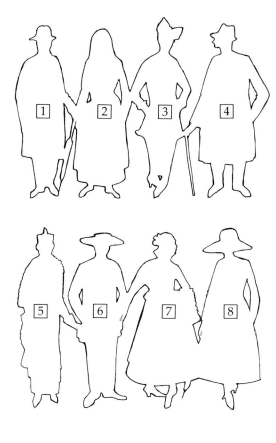

C. 1914–1917

[1] English gentleman *c*. 1914: trilby; double-breasted, knee-length coat of waterproof wool with large patch pockets; trousers with centre creases and turn-ups; leather gloves and shoes; umbrella.
[2] English nurse *c*. 1914: cotton veil; uniform dress with high round neckline, yoke, sleeves gathered at wrist and ankle-length skirt; apron with waistband and single patch pocket, the bib pinned to dress yoke; leather button boots with low heels. [3] French lady *c*. 1914: hat decorated with outsized pleated bow; fur-trimmed wool coat with double-breasted fastening in sets of four and yoke seam continued into fitted sleeves; low hip-belt; draped wrap-around skirt; silk stockings; leather gloves and shoes. [4] German gentleman *c*. 1915: trilby; knee-length coat with concealed fastening; breast pocket with silk handkerchief; two flap pockets; top-stitched detail on collar, revers, front panel and hem; narrow trousers with centre creases and turn-ups; leather gloves and shoes; walking stick.

[5] American lady *c*. 1916: brimless hat swathed with fabric and trimmed with feather and brooch; double fox-fur stole; jacket with buttons from collar to hem and contrasting bindings; high waist-belt; tiered skirt; leather gloves; handbag; button boots. [6] American man *c*. 1916: straw boater; shirt with round collar; striped necktie; waistcoat; matching jacket and narrow trousers; leather shoes.
[7] American lady *c*. 1916: brimless cloche hat trimmed with silk flowers; short jacket with wing collar and long tight sleeves; dress with high waist and full gathered skirt trimmed with bands of ribbon; silk stockings; leather shoes with high heels and instep straps; large fur muff. [8] English lady *c*. 1917: hat with wide brim and large crown swathed with silk chiffon; linen suit, the jacket with wide pin-tucked collar and long tight sleeves trimmed with straps and buttons to match hem of full skirt; high waist-belt; leather gloves and button boots with high heels; umbrella.

C. 1917–1920

[1] Englishman *c*. 1917: trilby; striped wool suit, the jacket with high button fastening, breast pocket with silk handkerchief and two flap pockets; trousers with centre creases; leather shoes. [2] French-woman *c*. 1917: golfing costume: straw boater; long shirt blouse with front buttons, large collar and long sleeves with cuff; wide sash tied around the waist; mid-calf-length gathered skirt; woollen stockings; leather golf shoes. [3] American woman *c*. 1918: felt hat with small brim, trimmed with ribbon band and feather; three-quarter-length coat with fur collar and cuffs, dolman sleeves, gathers from high yoke seam and flap pockets; high-heeled, leather button boots.
[4] Frenchwoman *c*. 1918: large straw hat; striped cotton dress with wide neckline, large collar and long sleeves with flared cuffs; bodice decorated with two rows of covered buttons; ankle-length skirt gathered over hips and caught into band above hem; leather button boots.

[5] Frenchwoman *c*. 1919: brimless hat with feather trim; mid-calf-length coat, the hem trimmed with fur to match large collar and cuffs; high waist-belt; narrow skirt; leather button boots.
[6] Frenchman *c*. 1919: bowler hat; double-breasted light wool suit with two flap pockets; breast pocket with silk handkerchief; narrow trousers with centre creases; leather gloves and shoes. [7] American woman *c*. 1920: hair dressed with false curls; bead earrings and necklace; silk dress with low round neckline and floating side panels; infill edged with lace; flared elbow-length sleeves; silk stockings; leather shoes with high heels and buckle trim. [8] Englishman *c*. 1920: trilby; waterproof wool overcoat with narrow collar, revers and raglan sleeves; self-fabric waist-belt with covered buckle; narrow trousers; leather gloves and shoes; walking stick.

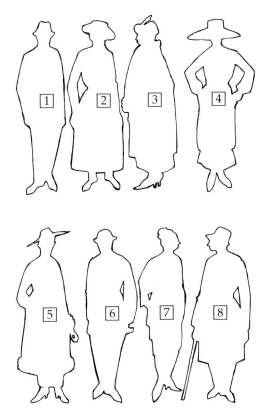

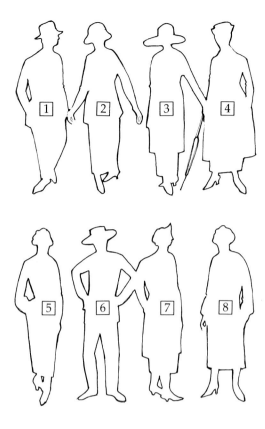

C. 1920–1923

[1] American man *c*. 1920: trilby; shirt and tie; double-breasted wool jacket with welt pockets and covered buttons; narrow flannel trousers with centre creases and turn-ups; leather shoes.
[2] American woman *c*. 1920: felt hat with deep crown and turned-down brim, decorated with contrasting colour felt strips; long linen jacket with high waist seam, flap pockets, long cuff sleeves and braid trimming; open neck blouse worn over wide collar and revers; ankle-length skirt; silk stockings; leather shoes. [3] Englishwoman *c*. 1921: straw hat with wide brim and high crown swathed with fine silk; knee-length jacket; stand collar, yoke, covered side buttons, belt and cuffs in contrasting colour to match narrow ankle-length skirt; leather boots; umbrella. [4] American woman *c*. 1921: felt hat with deep upturned brim decorated with felt flowers; knee-length heavy wool coat with high collar, side fastening, half belt, large patch pockets and top-stitched detail; narrow mid-calf-length skirt; silk stockings; leather shoes with instep straps.

[5] American woman *c*. 1921: short waved hair; fine silk blouse with large lace-edged collar and matching cuffs; mid-calf-length skirt with deep waistband and side pockets; lace-up leather shoes.
[6] Englishman *c*. 1922: straw boater with tall crown; double-breasted suit of lightweight wool with buttoned patch pockets; narrow trousers with centre creases and turn-ups; leather shoes.
[7] American waitress *c*. 1923: short waved hair; small pleated cap; mid-calf-length dress with lace-edged collar and cuffs; cotton overapron with low neckline and deep armholes, the gathered skirt with patch pockets falling from low-placed waistband; cotton stockings; leather shoes. [8] German woman *c*. 1923: short curled and waved hair; double Peter Pan collar and large bow; mid-calf-length dress with high yoke seam, full sleeves, cuffs and pleated skirt; low waist-belt; silk stockings; leather shoes.

C. 1924–1926

[1] Frenchwoman *c*. 1924: hair set into waves; lounging pyjamas of fine silk printed with outsized leaves; wide neckline; flared sleeves; hem and side split bound with contrasting colour of silk to match hip-belt and ankle-length pyjama trousers; silk stockings; satin mules with high heels. [2] American woman *c*. 1924: riding costume: bowler hat; hair in snood; shirt and tie; waistcoat; tailored jacket with breast and flap pockets; fitted breeches; long leather boots.
[3] American woman *c*. 1924: short hair set in waves; lightweight wool dress with tailored belt on hipline; buttoned inset in contrasting colour to match cuffs on fitted sleeves; skirt with side pleats; silk stockings; leather shoes. [4] American man *c*. 1925: trilby with wide brim; mid-calf-length, double-breasted fur coat with welt pockets and deep cuffs; narrow trousers; leather shoes.

[5] Frenchwoman *c*. 1925: short hair set into waves; bead necklace; knitted wool suit, the jacket with buttons from the neck to the hip and contrasting bands of knitting on waist, hip and wrist; knee-length pleated skirt; silk stockings; leather shoes with decorative straps. [6] Englishman *c*. 1925: golfing costume: peaked cap; shirt and tie; knitted jumper with V-shaped neckline and bands of pattern on the chest, upper and lower sleeves and waist; checked wool knickerbockers; knee-length knitted socks; leather shoes.
[7] German woman *c*. 1926: brimless cloche hat trimmed with wide band and rosette; knee-length dress with collar, front panel and cuffs of contrasting fabric and inset pipings on sleeves and bodice; tailored hip-belt; silk stockings; leather shoes. [8] Frenchwoman *c*. 1926: short straight hair with fringe; drop earrings and long necklace; sleeveless dress with square neckline; bloused bodice to hip, covered with lace from yoke to hip; matching falls of lace over skirt; silk flower decoration on hip; large feather fan; T-strap shoes.

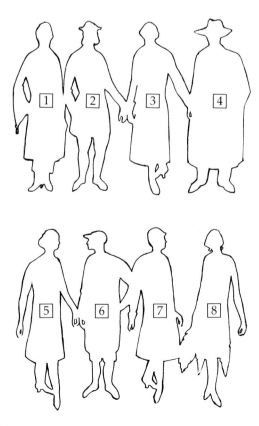

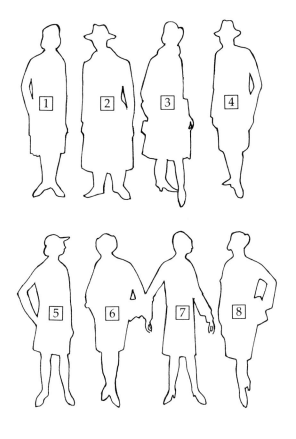

C. 1927–1930

1 German woman *c.* 1927: felt cloche hat; blouse with wide collar; knitted jumper with low round neckline and long sleeves; hip-length knitted jacket and pleated skirt. 2 American man *c.* 1927: trilby; mid-calf-length, double-breasted overcoat with fur collar, large patch and flap pockets and buttoned belt; narrow trousers with centre creases and turn-ups; leather gloves and shoes. 3 Frenchwoman *c.* 1928: cloche hat with upturned brim; glass bead earrings and necklace; knee-length coat with fur collar; matching fur cuffs; dress with low V-shaped neckline bound with contrasting colour; matching band on hip; tailored belt; knee-length pleated skirt; silk stockings; matching leather gloves; clutch bag; shoes with cross-over straps. 4 American man *c.* 1928: trilby; shirt and tie; waistcoat with four pockets; jacket with wide collar, revers and patch pockets; knickerbockers; knitted knee-socks; leather shoes.

5 Frenchwoman *c.* 1928: tennis wear: stiffened linen visor; tennis dress with collar, revers, cap sleeves, low waistline and knee-length pleated skirt; silk stockings; canvas lace-up shoes. 6 Englishwoman *c.* 1929: cloche hat with split brim; bead necklace; knee-length coat with long fur collar; matching fur trim on sleeves; low-placed pockets with stitched decoration and button trim echoed on hem of sleeves; leather envelope-shaped bag; leather shoes.
7 Frenchwoman *c.* 1929: straw cloche hat trimmed with felt leaves; knee-length crêpe de chine dress with wide square neckline bound with contrasting colour to match bands on hipline and wrist; wrap-around skirt; silk stockings; leather shoes with buckle. 8 English-woman *c.* 1930: cloche hat with upturned brim; bead earrings and necklace; knee-length coat with wide revers, two button fastening and raglan sleeves pleated into button at wrist; leather gloves, handbag and shoes.

C. 1930–1932

1 American man *c.* 1930: cotton shirt; silk tie with matching pocket handkerchief; three-piece suit including double-breasted waistcoat, jacket with flap pockets, wide trousers with centre creases and turn-ups; leather shoes. 2 Englishman *c.* 1930: shirt worn with bow tie; matching pocket handkerchief; double-breasted jacket; wide flannel trousers with centre creases and turn-ups; leather shoes.
3 American woman *c.* 1930: short permed hair; striped cotton blouse with short cuffed sleeves and patch pockets; neck scarf threaded through loop above the bust; ankle-length trousers with pointed yoke seam and large patch pockets with buttoned flaps; lace-up leather shoes with high heels. 4 English maid *c.* 1930: pleated cap; cotton dress with buttons from neck to hem; cotton Peter Pan collar and matching sleeve cuffs; bib apron with lace edging; cotton stockings; leather shoes with instep straps.

5 American woman *c.* 1931: waterproof rain hat; matching knee-length coat with raglan sleeves, strap fastening at wrist and large patch pockets; belt on natural waist; silk stockings; ankle-boots with turned-down cuffs, high heels and zip fastening. 6 Frenchwoman *c.* 1931: felt peaked cap with felt trim; mid-calf-length, double-breasted coat with fur collar and matching trim on flared cuffs; self-fabric belt with bow trim on natural waist; narrow skirt; leather gloves, handbag and shoes. 7 Englishwoman *c.* 1932: straw hat with wide brim; mid-calf-length coat with large fur collar; sleeves gathered into deep buttoned cuffs; double-breasted fastening with four large buttons; pockets set into seam on hip; leather shoes.
8 Frenchwoman *c.* 1932: short permed hair; couture dress of striped wool, the neckline wide with bias-cut scarf secured by brooch; matching bias-cut sleeves, bodice and skirt panels; tailored belt on natural waist; silk stockings; leather shoes.

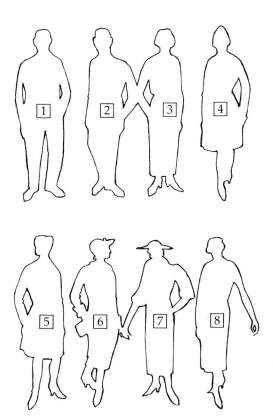

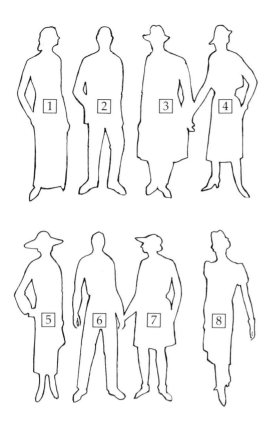

C. 1933–1936

1 American woman c. 1933: hair set into waves and dressed into a bun in nape of neck; bias-cut, silk satin evening dress, the low V-shaped neckline beaded on one side to match asymmetric seam from waist to hip; the full-length skirt with inset side panels; long gloves; small evening purse; satin sandals. 2 Englishman c. 1933: shirt and tie; knitted pullover with long sleeves; tweed jacket with patch pockets; wool trousers with centre creases and turn-ups; leather shoes. 3 American man c. 1934: trilby; double-breasted raincoat with wide collar, revers, belt with covered buckle and large patch pockets; straight-cut trousers with creases and turn-ups; leather gloves and shoes. 4 Englishwoman c. 1934: felt hat with pleated crown; clip-on earrings; pearl necklace; bolero jacket with edges bound in fabric of dress; silk dress with pleated skirt and low round neckline bound in fabric of bolero jacket to match belt; leather shoes.

5 Frenchwoman c. 1934: straw hat with wide brim, trimmed with ribbon and buckle; couture jacket of spotted silk with large collar, outsized bow and bishop sleeves; waist-belt with decorative clasp; matching silk, mid-calf-length skirt; silk stockings; leather shoes trimmed with bow. 6 Frenchman c. 1935: tennis wear: knitted cotton shirt with collar, short strap opening and short sleeves; wide flannel trousers with threaded belt, centre creases and turn-ups; lace-up canvas shoes. 7 Frenchwoman c. 1935: tennis wear: short permed hair; canvas visor on elasticated strap; sleeveless cotton blouse with pointed collar and strap opening to waist; knee-length, pleated linen skirt with button-trimmed pockets; knitted cotton ankle-socks; lace-up canvas shoes. 8 Englishwoman c. 1936: small, felt, brimless hat; crêpe de chine blouse with puff sleeves, the Peter Pan collar edged with fine pleats; sleeveless bolero decorated with felt flowers; straight skirt with wide box pleats; leather gloves with pointed cuffs; matching handbag and shoes.

C. 1936–1940

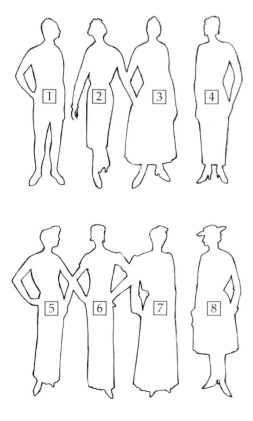

1 American woman c. 1936: bathing costume: fitted, rubber bathing cap with chin strap; knitted cotton bathing costume with narrow shoulder straps; ruched detail on bust; fitted bodice and hip-length skirt with built-in knickers; narrow belt; flat rubber pumps.
2 Frenchwoman c. 1937: short permed hair; striped wool dress with large, double organza collar and cuffs; wide suede belt with covered buckle to match bows above bust and over hip pleats; leather sandals with high heels. 3 Englishwoman c. 1938: silk turban; drop earrings; ankle-length, taffeta evening dress covered with fine silk net; narrow shoulder straps; neckline of fitted and ruched bodice edged with tiny pleats; narrow belt with clasp; full skirt; long gloves; satin sandals with high heels. 4 Englishwoman c. 1938: hair dressed in curls on top of head; sequin-embroidered, ankle-length dress with high round neckline, long sleeves, cut-away detail at neck and straight skirt with side split; gold kid shoes with high heels.

5 Frenchwoman c. 1939: hair dressed in roll over forehead; bias-cut, silk satin evening dress with wide shoulder straps, cross-over bodice and asymmetric drapery from one hip; satin sandals. 6 Englishwoman c. 1939: hair dressed in formal curls; fine wool crêpe evening dress with padded shoulders and short sleeves; embroidered inset on neckline and waistband; floor-length skirt with knife-pleated front panel; leather sandals. 7 American woman c. 1940: striped wool evening dress with shirt collar, yoke and padded shoulders; sleeves gathered into cuff; buttons from neck to waist; draped belt with buckle; full-length, knife-pleated skirt; leather sandals.
8 Englishwoman c. 1940: small straw hat trimmed with spotted silk; matching dress with bow tie at neck; pocket handkerchief; gauntlets; coat with padded shoulders, long tight sleeves and hip pockets; waist-belt; suede shoes with peep toes.

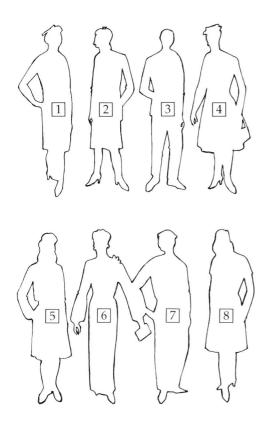

C. 1940–1943

[1] Englishwoman *c.* 1940: small brimless hat with bow trim and net veil; pearl earrings, necklace and bracelet; rayon dress with low V-shaped neckline; three-quarter-length sleeves; shaped seam with gathers under bust; narrow tailored belt; draped panel from side hip; long gloves; suede shoes with sandal fronts and ankle straps. [2] Englishwoman *c.* 1940: brimless hat trimmed with felt leaves; hip-length jacket with small Peter Pan collar, padded shoulders, long tight sleeves and gathered patch pockets set into side panel seams; knee-length flared skirt; leather shoes. [3] Englishman *c.* 1941: evening wear: shirt with wing collar; bow tie; waistcoat with shawl collar; tailcoat with wide revers faced with silk; wide trousers with centre creases; leather spats. [4] Englishwoman *c.* 1942: pill-box hat trimmed with wide bow; knee-length dress with high round neckline and V-shaped cut-out detail; padded shoulders; long tight sleeves with narrow cuff; tailored belt; skirt with gathered side panels.

[5] American woman *c.* 1942: long hair dressed into large waves and rolls; wool shirt blouse with pointed collar, tucks each side of button opening, padded shoulders and sleeves gathered into cuff; pinafore dress with low square neckline and patch pockets; waistband decorated with buttons; flared skirt with inverted box pleat; ankle-socks; shoes with crêpe soles. [6] American woman *c.* 1942: long, wool crêpe evening dress with low V-shaped neckline and ruched detail; padded shoulders; bishop sleeves; tailored belt; skirt with single knife pleat; satin purse and matching sandals; corsage of silk flowers on shoulder. [7] Englishman *c.* 1943: tweed cap; shirt and tie; long-sleeved pullover with high round neck, trimmed with patterned bands across the chest and waist; wide trousers with turn-ups; leather shoes. [8] American woman *c.* 1943: long hair dressed into large waves and rolls; knee-length dress with bow tie, Peter Pan collar, cuffed short sleeves and decorative seams and pleats.

C. 1944–1947

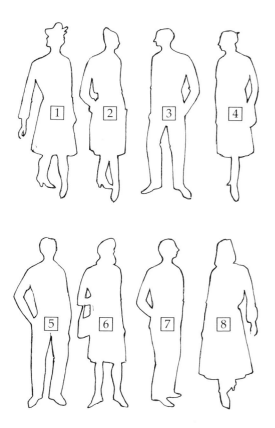

[1] Englishwoman *c.* 1944: small felt hat with twisted crown, trimmed with self felt loop; knee-length, double-breasted wool coat with high collar, padded shoulders and decorative seam from yoke to hip pleat, the sleeves gathered into a cuff; wide belt with large buckle; leather gloves, handbag and shoes. [2] American woman *c.* 1944: small brimless hat with pointed crown; wool dress with narrow Peter Pan collar and long sleeves; matching tailored belt; side panels of bodice and knee-length skirt in contrasting colour; leather gauntlets; leather shoes with buckle trim. [3] Englishman *c.* 1945: knitted pullover with high round neck and long raglan sleeves; wide trousers with turn-ups; leather shoes. [4] American woman *c.* 1946: skull cap with wired stalk; striped cotton dress with small, plain cotton shirt collar, half yoke, padded shoulders and short sleeves; tailored leather belt; knee-length skirt with centre front pleat and large patch pockets; leather shoulder bag, gloves and shoes.

[5] American man *c.* 1946: striped cotton shirt with collar worn open and short sleeves with stitched cuffs; wide linen trousers with deep waistband and turn-ups; leather belt; leather shoes. [6] Englishwoman *c.* 1946: beret; blouse with small collar and tied bow; striped wool jacket with padded shoulders, single-breasted fastening and top-stitched side panels with pockets; pleated skirt; leather handbag and gloves; shoes with wedge heels, platform soles and peep toes. [7] Englishman *c.* 1947: silk neck scarf; checked wool jacket with patch pockets; flannel trousers; leather shoes. [8] Frenchwoman *c.* 1947: rainproof, wool gaberdine coat with large hood, double-breasted fastening and buttoned belt; the mid-calf-length full skirt with large flap and patch pockets; leather gloves.

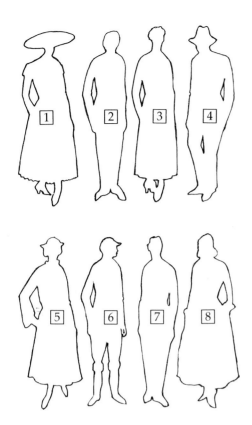

C. 1947–1950

1 Frenchwoman *c.* 1947: large straw hat; silk taffeta couture dress with wide neckline and draped collar; fitted bodice; buttons from neck to belted waist; three-quarter-length sleeves; mid-calf-length, pleated skirt with tucked and stitched hip yoke; nylon stockings; leather shoes. 2 American man *c.* 1948: double-breasted jacket with piped and flap pockets; wide belt; corduroy trousers; suede ankle-boots. 3 Englishwoman *c.* 1948: rayon cocktail dress with sweetheart neckline; padded shoulders; long tight sleeves; fitted bodice; shaded hip seam; mid-calf-length skirt, the inset pocket decorated with buttons to match wrist and neckline; leather sandals with high heels. 4 American man *c.* 1949: panama hat; casual shirt worn open at neck; knitted waistcoat; striped linen suit, the jacket with piped pockets, the wide trousers with turn-ups; suede and leather slippers.

5 Englishwoman *c.* 1949: small felt hat; mid-calf-length checked wool coat with large collar, edge-to-edge hook fastening and dart on outer bodice; long flared sleeves; full skirt; wide suede belt; leather gloves and shoes. 6 American man *c.* 1949: hunting costume: close-fitting peaked cap; knitted shirt; checked wool jacket with leather yoke, faced revers, buttons and inset flap pockets; knitted collar, sleeve cuffs and welt pockets; matching breeches; long knitted socks; waterproof boots laced from instep to knee. 7 Frenchman *c.* 1950: knitted cotton shirt; silk tie; casual linen jacket with yoke seam, large patch pockets, covered buttons and belt; wide linen trousers with turn-ups; suede slippers. 8 American woman *c.* 1950: long waved hair; rayon taffeta dress with low sweetheart neckline and fitted bodice; fine lace infill; three-quarter-length sleeves with cuffs; velvet belt trimmed with silk flower; mid-calf-length circular skirt; nylon stockings; leather shoes with high heels.

C. 1950–1953

1 Englishman *c.* 1950: casual jacket with narrow collar, revers, raglan sleeves, two breast pockets and two patch and flap pockets; belt; cotton corduroy trousers with turn-ups; leather shoes.
2 American woman *c.* 1950: straw hat with small crown and wide brim; dress with wide off-the-shoulder neckline, the collar with bound edge in contrasting colour to match tailored belt and hem binding on full skirt; fitted bodice; three-quarter-length sleeves; cotton gloves; leather handbag and shoes. 3 Englishman *c.* 1951: knee-length, single-breasted raincoat with flap and patch pockets and top-stitched edges and seams; wide trousers; leather gloves and shoes. 4 Frenchwoman *c.* 1951: small hat with draped crown; silk neck scarf; princess-line, mid-calf-length coat with wide shawl collar and two-button fastening on waist; long tight sleeves with cuffs; full skirt; leather gloves and shoes.

5 Frenchwoman *c.* 1952: brimless felt hat with single feather trim; hip-length checked wool jacket with two deep box pleats; narrow plain wool skirt with short back vent; nylon stockings; leather shoes with high heels. 6 American woman *c.* 1952: short permed hair; pearl earrings and necklace; rayon dress with off-the-shoulder neckline, deep collar, fitted bodice with ruched detail and mid-calf-length full skirt; leather shoes with high heels and peep toes.
7 Frenchwoman *c.* 1953: beach costume: large straw hat; short bodice with halter neck and cuffed neck edge; shorts with turn-ups; large beach bag with scarf tied to handle; flat leather sandals.
8 Englishwoman *c.* 1953: tennis wear: sleeveless, cotton tennis dress with front zip fastening and short pleated skirt; narrow tailored belt; cotton ankle-socks; canvas lace-up shoes.

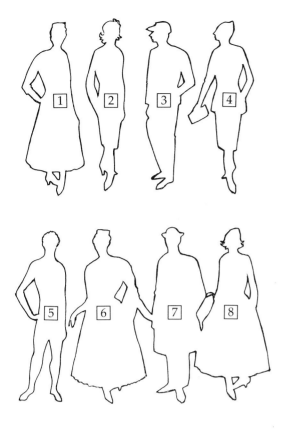

C. 1953–1956

[1] Englishwoman *c.* 1953: small pill-box hat; double-breasted velvet jacket with low round neckline and three-quarter-length sleeves; taffeta dress with Peter Pan collar and band of velvet inserted above hem of mid-calf-length full skirt; long gloves; nylon stockings; leather shoes. [2] Frenchwoman *c.* 1954: small brimless hat with feather trim; dress with checked wool bodice and three-quarter-length sleeves, the narrow plain wool skirt with hip pockets; long leather gloves; large leather handbag; leather shoes with high heels. [3] Englishman *c.* 1954: double-breasted jacket with brass buttons, large patch pockets and breast pocket with silk handkerchief to match neck tie; flannel trousers; suede shoes. [4] Englishwoman *c.* 1954: small, brimless felt hat; fine wool suit, the hip-length, double-breasted jacket with three-quarter-length sleeves, small collar and revers; silk scarf; brooch; narrow skirt; long gloves; leather handbag and shoes.

[5] Englishwoman *c.* 1955: short permed hair; spotted cotton bikini bra top with halter straps; matching hip-length skirt with built-in knickers; flat sandals covered in matching fabric. [6] Frenchwoman *c.* 1955: small pill-box hat with bow trim; strapless, chiffon evening dress with draped bodice, the ankle-length full skirt worn over stiffened petticoats; silk flowers pinned at waist; chiffon stole; short satin gloves; matching shoes with low heels and peep toes. [7] Englishman *c.* 1956: bowler hat; overcoat with velvet collar, concealed front opening, breast pocket with silk handkerchief and flap pockets; wool trousers with narrow stripe; leather gloves and shoes; rolled umbrella. [8] Englishwoman *c.* 1956: cotton dress with boned bodice, shoulder straps and waist-sash, the mid-calf-length full skirt worn over stiffened petticoats; leather shoes with low heels.

C. 1956–1959

[1] American woman *c.* 1956: rayon blouse with wing collar and short sleeves with flared cuff; wide plastic belt; circular-cut felt skirt embroidered with garlands of flowers; sandals with low heels. [2] American woman *c.* 1956: sleeveless, spotted cotton dress with low square neckline and fitted bodice with hip seam; the skirt with two inverted box pleats topped with bows; leather shoes with stiletto heels. [3] American woman *c.* 1957: scarf tied around neck; knitted cotton blouse with wide off-the-shoulder neckline and fitted bodice; wide elasticated belt with clasp fastening at front; pedal pushers; flat leather pumps. [4] Englishman *c.* 1957: shirt with concealed fastening worn with bow tie; silk and mohair evening suit, the jacket with silk-faced shawl collar and bound pockets; narrow trousers.

[5] Frenchwoman *c.* 1958: wool dress with slashed neckline and short dolman sleeves; decorative bow under bust; pockets on hipline; leather shoes with cross-over straps and high stiletto heels. [6] Englishwoman *c.* 1958: straw hat with upturned brim, bound with ribbon; collarless jacket with elbow-length sleeves, large suede buttons, hip band and bow tie; narrow skirt; long gloves; leather handbag and shoes. [7] Frenchwoman *c.* 1958: strapless, chiffon evening dress, the boned bodice draped with chiffon; the skirt gathered at waist and into a band at knee, supported over petticoats of same shape; long stretch satin gloves; satin shoes with pointed toes and stiletto heels. [8] Frenchwoman *c.* 1959: small pill-box hat covered in dress fabric; matching earrings and necklace; knee-length dress with high waist seam trimmed with large bow; slashed neckline; short sleeves; flared skirt; long leather gloves; shoes with ankle straps, pointed toes and stiletto heels. [9] Frenchwoman *c.* 1959: grosgrain couture evening dress; fitted boned bodice with halter neck and bow trim on bust; flared skirt; long gloves.

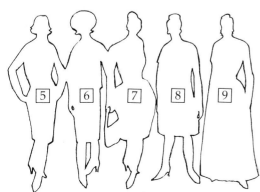

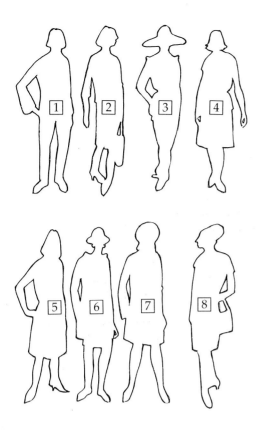

C. 1960-1964

1 Englishwoman *c*. 1960: rayon shirt blouse with pointed collar and long sleeves; hip-length, sleeveless suede jerkin with low square neckline and half belt with button trim; ankle-length drainpipe trousers; flat leather pumps. 2 American woman *c*. 1960: wide hair band; short straight hair; wool suit, the collarless jacket with high round neckline, three-quarter-length sleeves, single suede button fastening to match bow at waist; narrow knee-length skirt; short leather gloves; leather handbag and shoes. 3 Englishwoman *c*. 1961: large straw hat; sleeveless beach top with wide neckline and frilled edge; matching gathered hem on shorts; wide plastic belt with buckle; beach mules. 4 Englishwoman *c*. 1961: knitted wool jersey, hip-length top with wide neckline, short sleeves and straight bodice gathered at waist; flared skirt; nylon stockings; leather shoes with pointed toes, high stiletto heels and short instep straps.

5 Englishwoman *c*. 1963: sleeveless cotton sundress with boat-shaped neckline open each side from underarm to hipline; strap and button fastening; flared knee-length skirt; nylon stockings; leather sling-back shoes with low heels and pointed toes. 6 Frenchwoman *c*. 1964: straw hat with wide band; double-breasted wool coat with wide neckline, narrow collar, flap pockets and three-quarter-length sleeves with button and strap; short straight skirt; long plastic boots; short cotton gloves. 7 Englishwoman *c*. 1964: straw hat with turned-back brim; knee-length wool coat with high button fastening, narrow collar and revers; four buttoned patch pockets; flared skirt; long sleeves with cuff; nylon tights; leather shoes with wide, diagonal instep strap. 8 American woman *c*. 1964: domed felt hat; short hair; dress with low scooped neckline; short dolman sleeves bound in contrasting colour; bow at waist; narrow skirt; short gloves; large plastic handbag; matching plastic shoes with low heels and pointed toes.

C. 1965-1967

1 Englishwoman *c*. 1965: false hair pieces; large plastic earrings; silk evening pyjamas; hip-length sleeveless top with high round halter neck and beaded edge to match hem; bow-trimmed belt under bust; flared trousers; satin boots. 2 Italian man *c*. 1966: small trilby; knee-length coat with raglan sleeves, concealed fastening, welt and patch pockets and top-stitching; narrow trousers; lace-up suede shoes. 3 Frenchwoman *c*. 1966: hair dressed in high knot; large drop earrings; full-length, silk satin evening dress with high beaded yoke to match cuffs of bishop sleeves; satin pumps.
4 Englishwoman *c*. 1966: peaked leather cap; wool gaberdine, mini-length coat with high round neckline, flat collar, yoke, patch pockets and sleeves with buttoned strap; nylon tights; flat leather pumps with button trim.

5 Italian man *c*. 1967: silk shirt; large velvet bow tie; mohair and silk striped evening jacket with silk-faced lapels and bound pockets; silk pocket handkerchief; straight-cut trousers; suede ankle-boots.
6 Englishwoman *c*. 1967: short straight hair with false piece and ribbon decoration; polo-neck jumper; mini-length dress with front zip fastening, wide collar, three-quarter-length sleeves and flared skirt with inverted box pleat; nylon tights; flat leather pumps.
7 Frenchwoman *c*. 1967: velvet peaked cap; heavy wool trouser suit; jacket with stand collar, shaped yoke, front side panels, front zip fastening, sleeve cuffs, hip band and decorative top-stitching; narrow trousers; leather ankle-boots. 8 Italian man *c*. 1967: suede jacket with knitted collar and cuffs; concealed fastenings under strap decorated with covered buttons at neck and hip; yoke seam with inset pockets; vertical bound pockets; trousers flared from knee; leather ankle-boots.

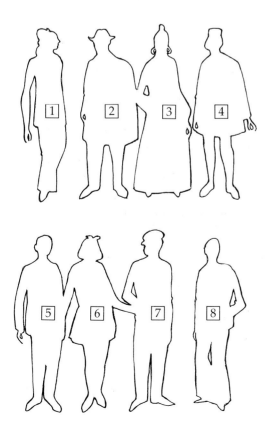

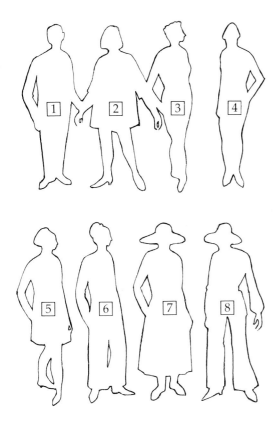

C. 1967–1969

[1] Frenchman *c.* 1967: cotton shirt; striped silk tie; cotton corduroy jacket with high button fastening and buttoned flap pockets; straight wool trousers; leather shoes. [2] American woman *c.* 1968: hair piece attached to Alice band; mini-length, silk evening dress; stand collar, slit neckline, armholes, hem of both elbow-length sleeves and skirt embroidered with beads; flared sleeves decorated with clusters of beads; nylon tights; patent leather shoes with low heels. [3] Frenchwoman *c.* 1968: short curly wig; stretch nylon bathing costume, the halter neck bound with bands of contrasting colour; towelling mules. [4] Frenchwoman *c.* 1968: short wig with pointed fringe; elasticated cotton bathing costume, the neckband attached to the bra and the bra to the mini-skirt with built-in knickers; leather sandals.

[5] Frenchwoman *c.* 1968: false hair piece attached to Alice band; sleeveless silk mini dress with deep collar edged with decorative top-stitching; matching side panel seams and pleats; nylon tights; leather shoes with low heels and square toes. [6] American woman *c.* 1969: false hair pieces; large bead earrings; silk evening pyjamas; the high round neckline and long centre split edged with braid to match cuffs of long tight sleeves, pointed hem of bodice and hem of wide flared trousers; satin shoes with low heels. [7] Englishwoman *c.* 1969: large felt hat with swathed crown; polo-neck jumper; mid-calf-length, double-breasted coat with half round yoke, flap pockets, leather buttons, binding and trimming; long leather boots. [8] Englishwoman *c.* 1969: large felt hat; hip-length safari jacket with large collar and deep yoke; sleeves gathered into cuffs; tie belt; large patch and flap pockets; matching bell bottoms; leather boots with high heels.

C. 1970–1972

[1] Frenchman *c.* 1970: short, heavy wool overcoat with top-stitching on yoke seam, collar and revers, patch and bound pockets; wool gaberdine flared trousers; leather boots. [2] Italian woman *c.* 1970: silk turban; hip-length silk blouse with wide neckline and centre split; decorative braid, loop and button fastening; narrow cord belt; bishop sleeves; trousers tucked into long leather boots. [3] Frenchwoman *c.* 1970: silk evening pyjamas; hip-length top with wide neckline trimmed with braids to match motif in centre of bodice and hem of flared sleeves; pocket set into panel seam; wide flared trousers; satin pumps. [4] American woman *c.* 1970: felt hat with tall crown and wide brim; long straight hair; long braid necklace; hip-length blouse gathered into waist with wide belt; round neckline, slit opening, sleeve cuffs and hem edged with braid; mid-calf-length flared skirt; long leather boots with high heels.

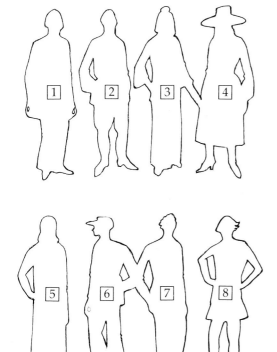

[5] American woman *c.* 1971: knitted polo-neck jumper; matching ankle-length trousers; mid-calf-length, sleeveless and collarless cardigan; button strap, armholes and welt of patch pockets in contrasting colour; leather mules with platform soles and high thick heels. [6] Englishwoman *c.* 1971: velvet cap; polo-neck jumper; double-breasted jacket with wide collar and revers, long tight sleeves and patch pockets; bell bottoms; leather boots with platform soles and high thick heels. [7] Frenchman *c.* 1972: polo-neck jumper; corduroy jacket with high button fastening, yoke, wide collar and revers, top-stitched strap, half belt and patch pockets; flared trousers; leather boots with platform soles and thick heels. [8] American woman *c.* 1972: short asymmetric hair cut; stretch cotton dress with bound halter neck and fitted hip-length bodice; wide leather belt; gathered mini-skirt; nylon tights; leather shoes with platform soles, high heels and peep toes.

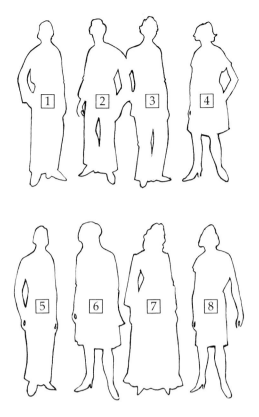

C. 1973–1976

1 Englishman *c.* 1973: polo-neck jumper; waist-length suede jacket with side zip fastening; sleeves with zipped cuffs; pockets with zip fastenings; wide waistband; flared trousers; leather boots with high heels and platform soles. 2 Englishwoman *c.* 1973: knitted cloche hat; blouse with wide collar and long sleeves gathered into deep cuffs; sleeveless knitted jumper tucked into bell bottoms; leather belt with round buckle; leather boots with high heels and platform soles. 3 American man *c.* 1974: short permed hair; silk neck scarf; double-breasted, striped wool jacket with flap pockets; flared wool trousers; leather boots with platform soles. 4 American woman *c.* 1974: wool crêpe dress with low V-shaped neckline; tie detail in self fabric; draped bodice; short bias-cut sleeves; knee-length flared skirt; leather shoes with high heels, ankle straps and peep toes.

5 Italian man *c.* 1975: polo-neck jumper; suede jacket with wide collar, revers and yoke; front zip fastening; wide belt; sloping zip pockets; wide flared trousers; leather boots with high heels and platform soles. 6 American woman *c.* 1975: straw hat with upturned brim; long bead necklace; blouse with wide pointed collar; cardigan jacket edges and cuffs bound in contrasting colour; knee-length pleated skirt; leather bag with long shoulder strap; nylon tights; leather shoes with high heels and ankle straps.
7 Englishwoman *c.* 1976: long permed hair; floor-length dress with high waist line; stand collar, sleeves and bodice decorated with cotton braid; gathered skirt with frill at hem and braid trim; leather boots with high heels. 8 Frenchwoman *c.* 1976: striped silk jersey dress; contrasting round neckline bound to match tie belt; yoke and cap sleeves cut in one; straight knee-length skirt; nylon tights; leather shoes with cross-over straps.

C. 1977–1980

1 Italian woman *c.* 1977: straw hat with wide ribbon band; shirt blouse; necktie; collarless, hip-length jacket with narrow tailored belt, padded shoulders and large patch pockets; knee-length flared skirt; nylon tights; leather shoes with high heels and ankle straps.
2 Italian man *c.* 1977: polo-neck jumper; rainproof casual jacket with hood, gathered at waist with cord; zip fastening; patch breast pockets and sloping bound pockets; narrow trousers; leather and suede slippers. 3 Italian man *c.* 1978: lightweight wool shirt with round collar; silk necktie tucked into button opening; wool gaberdine jacket with narrow collar, revers, two-button fastening and bound pockets; narrow trousers; leather shoes. 4 Englishwoman *c.* 1978: long hair; loop earrings; bead necklace; mixed-fabric smock top with V-shaped neckline, pleated fabric to hip and flared sleeves edged with braid; mixed-fabric, ankle-length skirt with hem frill; long leather boots with high heels.

5 Englishwoman *c.* 1979: wrapover dress with tie belt, shawl collar and three-quarter-length sleeves; nylon tights; leather sandals.
6 Italian man *c.* 1980: leather T-shirt tucked into narrow leather trousers with seams on knee; leather belt with metal buckle; leather jacket with rolled-up raglan sleeves, large shoulder pads, shawl collar and stud fastening; leather ankle-boots. 7 Englishwoman *c.* 1980: long permed hair; jersey dress with high round neckline, padded shoulders, long tight sleeves and fitted bodice; rouleau belt in three contrasting colours; mini-length skirt gathered from hip seam; nylon tights; leather shoes with low heels and wide instep straps. 8 Italian woman *c.* 1980: short hair; large plastic earrings and matching necklace; jacket with wide belt, padded shoulders, wide shawl collar and welt pockets; dress with short straight skirt; nylon tights; leather handbag and shoes.

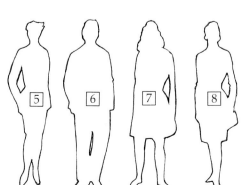

Illustrated Glossary of Terms

ALICE BAND   20th century. A band of fabric worn around a woman's head to keep the hair off the face. ☐1

BAG SLEEVE   15th and 16th centuries. A long, very full sleeve gathered into a wrist cuff. ☐2

BARBETTE   13th century to 16th century. White linen band covering a woman's neck and chin. ☐3

BELL BOTTOMS   20th century, particularly 1960s. Trousers with exaggerated flare from the knee to the hem.

BERTHA   19th and early 20th centuries. A woman's cape-like collar, usually of lace, covering the shoulders. ☐4

BIAS CUT   20th century. A cut diagonally across the grain of the fabric. Very popular in the 1920s and 1930s.

BICORN HAT   18th century. Alternative spelling: bicorne. Hat with the brim turned up on opposite sides to form two points. ☐5

BISHOP SLEEVE   19th and 20th centuries. A woman's long sleeve fitted to the elbow and then flaring out to the wrist. Usually caught into a cuff, though sometimes left loose. ☐6

BLOOMERS   Mid-19th and early 20th centuries. A woman's leg garment gathered at the knee or ankle. ☐7

BOATER   Late 19th century onwards. Flat-brimmed straw hat painted with shellac to harden the surface. ☐8

BOAT-SHAPED NECK   20th century. Also known as bateau neckline. A shallow, gently curved neckline cut from one shoulder to the other. It has the same appearance at the front and the back. ☐9

BOLERO   Late 19th century onwards. A short tailored jacket reaching almost to the waistline. Short or long sleeved or sleeveless. The jacket usually worn open. ☐10

BOOT HOSE   17th century. Protective linen stockings, worn by men under boots, with a wide lace cuff. ☐11

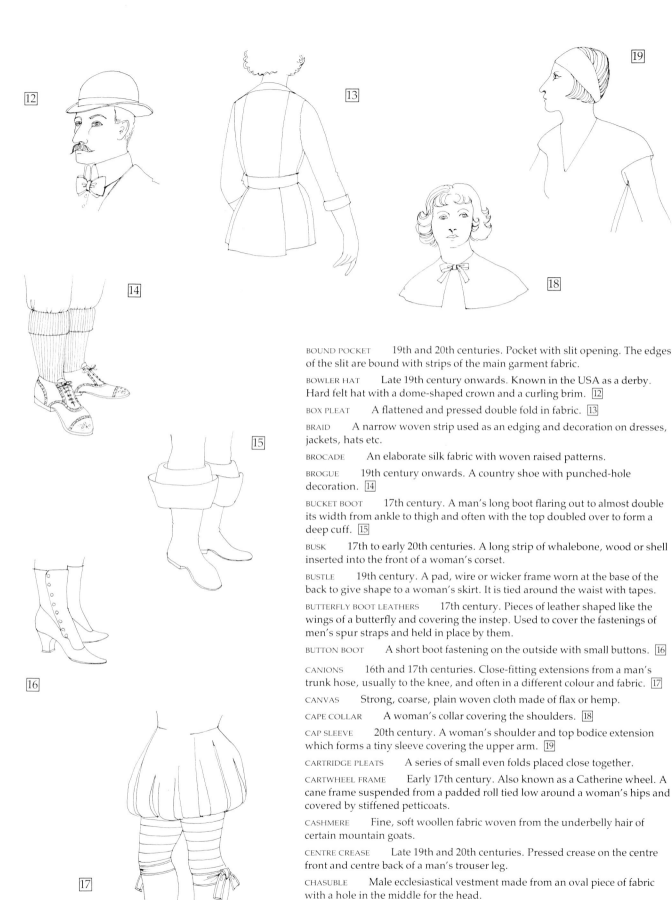

BOUND POCKET   19th and 20th centuries. Pocket with slit opening. The edges of the slit are bound with strips of the main garment fabric.

BOWLER HAT   Late 19th century onwards. Known in the USA as a derby. Hard felt hat with a dome-shaped crown and a curling brim. 12

BOX PLEAT   A flattened and pressed double fold in fabric. 13

BRAID   A narrow woven strip used as an edging and decoration on dresses, jackets, hats etc.

BROCADE   An elaborate silk fabric with woven raised patterns.

BROGUE   19th century onwards. A country shoe with punched-hole decoration. 14

BUCKET BOOT   17th century. A man's long boot flaring out to almost double its width from ankle to thigh and often with the top doubled over to form a deep cuff. 15

BUSK   17th to early 20th centuries. A long strip of whalebone, wood or shell inserted into the front of a woman's corset.

BUSTLE   19th century. A pad, wire or wicker frame worn at the base of the back to give shape to a woman's skirt. It is tied around the waist with tapes.

BUTTERFLY BOOT LEATHERS   17th century. Pieces of leather shaped like the wings of a butterfly and covering the instep. Used to cover the fastenings of men's spur straps and held in place by them.

BUTTON BOOT   A short boot fastening on the outside with small buttons. 16

CANIONS   16th and 17th centuries. Close-fitting extensions from a man's trunk hose, usually to the knee, and often in a different colour and fabric. 17

CANVAS   Strong, coarse, plain woven cloth made of flax or hemp.

CAPE COLLAR   A woman's collar covering the shoulders. 18

CAP SLEEVE   20th century. A woman's shoulder and top bodice extension which forms a tiny sleeve covering the upper arm. 19

CARTRIDGE PLEATS   A series of small even folds placed close together.

CARTWHEEL FRAME   Early 17th century. Also known as a Catherine wheel. A cane frame suspended from a padded roll tied low around a woman's hips and covered by stiffened petticoats.

CASHMERE   Fine, soft woollen fabric woven from the underbelly hair of certain mountain goats.

CENTRE CREASE   Late 19th and 20th centuries. Pressed crease on the centre front and centre back of a man's trouser leg.

CHASUBLE   Male ecclesiastical vestment made from an oval piece of fabric with a hole in the middle for the head.

CHEMISE   12th century onwards. A long or short shift usually worn by women next to the skin.

CHIFFON   A fine transparent material made from silk or synthetic yarns. Often used for evening wear.

CHITON   Ancient Greek times. A basic tunic falling to the ankle for women and to the knee for men.

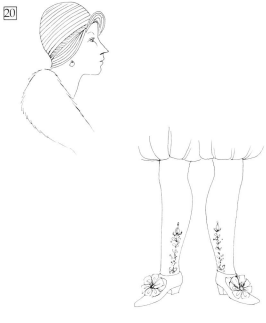

CIRCLET   A decorative headband made of either metal or fine fabric.

CIRCULAR SKIRT   20th century. A woman's skirt made from a complete circle of fabric.

CLOCHE HAT   20th century. A woman's close-fitting hat with or without a brim, covering the back of the neck and pulled well over the forehead. 20

CLOCKS   16th century onwards. Embroidered or woven decoration on the ankles of stockings. 21

CLUTCH BAG   20th century, 1930s onwards. A handbag without a handle or strap.

COCKADE   17th century onwards. An ornamental rosette of ribbon, sometimes with feathers, worn on a hat.

COCKTAIL DRESS   20th century. Usually a short dress made from luxurious fabric and worn in the early evening for parties, the theatre or dinner. 22

CODPIECE   15th and 16th centuries. The front flap of material joining a man's hose and forming a pouch. In the 16th century it was often padded and decorated with embroidery. 23

COIF   12th century to 15th century. Close-fitting bonnet covering the ears and tied under the chin. 24

CORDUROY   A thick cotton fabric, ribbed and with a velvet pile. Before the 20th century it was worn by servants and working people. During the 20th century it has been used mainly for casual wear.

CORSAGE   A small bouquet of flowers worn by women on the shoulder, bosom, waistband or wrist or pinned to a bag or muff.

CORSET   19th-century term for stays. A two-piece fitted underbodice fastening at the front with hooks and at the back with laces. Made from stiff heavy cotton or linen and cut in shaped panels. Metal or whalebone strips are inserted for extra rigidity. 25

COTEHARDIE   12th century to 14th century. Close-fitting outer garment falling to the hip for men and the ground for women. 26

COUTURE   Mid-19th century onwards. Abbreviation of the French *haute couture*. It is used to mean individually made and designed clothes.

COWL   a) 12th century to 14th century. Hood attached to a monk's robe or similar garment. b) 20th century. A folded and draped neckline on women's garments at the back or the front or both. 27

CRAVAT   17th century onwards. Stock, scarf or neck cloth. Any fabric tied around the neck and throat. 28

CRÊPE   Fabric with a soft crinkled texture.

CRÊPE DE CHINE   19th and 20th centuries. Fine fabric made from raw silk and used for blouses, lingerie, nightwear etc.

CRINOLINE   19th century. a) 1840s onwards. A woman's petticoat, corded and lined with horsehair. b) 1850s. A woman's petticoat of quilted cotton, reinforced with whalebone. c) 1860s. A cage-like construction of flexible steel hoops used to support women's skirts.

CUMMERBUND   a) Late 19th century. A man's waist-sash, sometimes worn instead of a waistcoat. b) 20th century. Used in women's fashion for both day and evening wear. ₂₉

DAGGING   14th century to 16th century. Ornamental edging. Edges cut into scallops, tongues or leaf shapes. ₃₀

DALMATIC   Ecclesiastical vestment. A knee-length robe with short wide sleeves.

DERBY   19th and 20th centuries. American term for a bowler hat.

DOLMAN SLEEVE   20th century. Sleeve cut in one piece with the bodice and often narrowing to the wrist when full length. ₃₁

DOUBLET   15th century to 17th century. A padded, close-fitting jacket worn over the skirt. Sometimes small skirts or tabs were added at the waist. ₃₂

DRAINPIPE TROUSERS   20th century. Trousers tapering from the knee to the ankle in a very tight fit.

DRAWERS   16th century onwards. Loose-fitting undergarments for lower trunk and legs. Length varies from knee to ankle according to the period in which they were worn.

EPAULETTE   Alternative spelling: epaulet. a) 16th and 17th centuries. An extension of stiffened or padded fabric set into the seam between the sleeve and the shoulder. b) 17th century onwards. A strip of fabric or knotted cord set upon the shoulder seam. Often trimmed with insignia or metal fringing. ₃₃

FICHU   18th and 19th centuries. Shawl or scarf of fine material or lace. Worn around the shoulders and tied or fastened over the breast. ₃₄

FILLET   Narrow headband tied at the back. Made of various materials.

FLANNEL   a) 18th to 20th centuries. Soft worsted woollen fabric. b) 19th century. Red flannel was a very popular fabric for both male and female underwear. c) 20th century. Mainly used for outerwear: trousers, jackets, coats and the like.

FLAP POCKET   A pocket slit and bound and covered with a top flap of fabric.

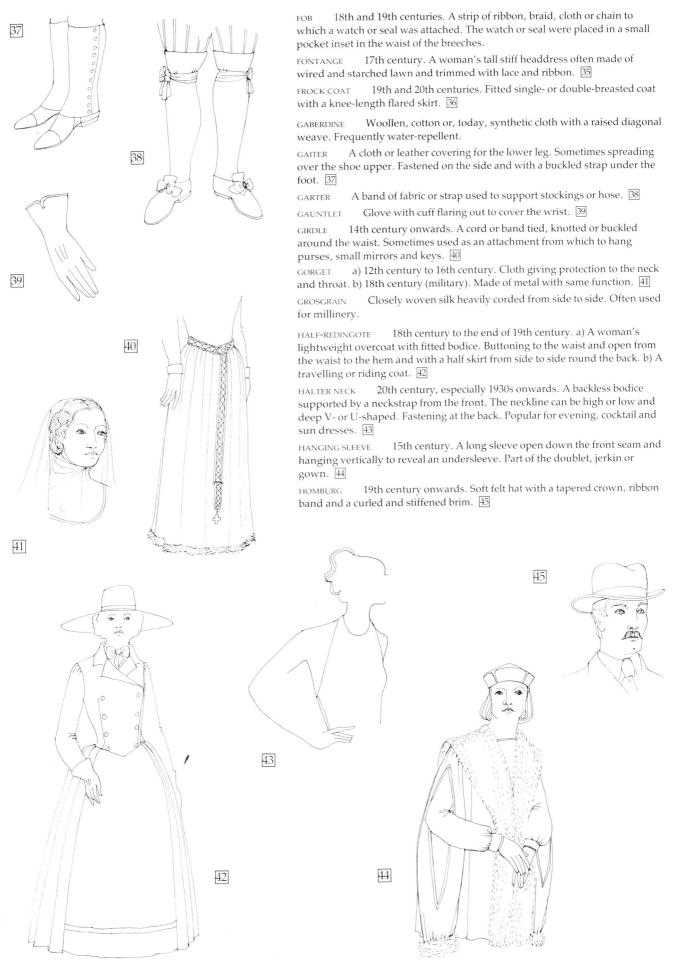

FOB 18th and 19th centuries. A strip of ribbon, braid, cloth or chain to which a watch or seal was attached. The watch or seal were placed in a small pocket inset in the waist of the breeches.

FONTANGE 17th century. A woman's tall stiff headdress often made of wired and starched lawn and trimmed with lace and ribbon. 35

FROCK COAT 19th and 20th centuries. Fitted single- or double-breasted coat with a knee-length flared skirt. 36

GABERDINE Woollen, cotton or, today, synthetic cloth with a raised diagonal weave. Frequently water-repellent.

GAITER A cloth or leather covering for the lower leg. Sometimes spreading over the shoe upper. Fastened on the side and with a buckled strap under the foot. 37

GARTER A band of fabric or strap used to support stockings or hose. 38

GAUNTLET Glove with cuff flaring out to cover the wrist. 39

GIRDLE 14th century onwards. A cord or band tied, knotted or buckled around the waist. Sometimes used as an attachment from which to hang purses, small mirrors and keys. 40

GORGET a) 12th century to 16th century. Cloth giving protection to the neck and throat. b) 18th century (military). Made of metal with same function. 41

GROSGRAIN Closely woven silk heavily corded from side to side. Often used for millinery.

HALF-REDINGOTE 18th century to the end of 19th century. a) A woman's lightweight overcoat with fitted bodice. Buttoning to the waist and open from the waist to the hem and with a half skirt from side to side round the back. b) A travelling or riding coat. 42

HALTER NECK 20th century, especially 1930s onwards. A backless bodice supported by a neckstrap from the front. The neckline can be high or low and deep V- or U-shaped. Fastening at the back. Popular for evening, cocktail and sun dresses. 43

HANGING SLEEVE 15th century. A long sleeve open down the front seam and hanging vertically to reveal an undersleeve. Part of the doublet, jerkin or gown. 44

HOMBURG 19th century onwards. Soft felt hat with a tapered crown, ribbon band and a curled and stiffened brim. 45

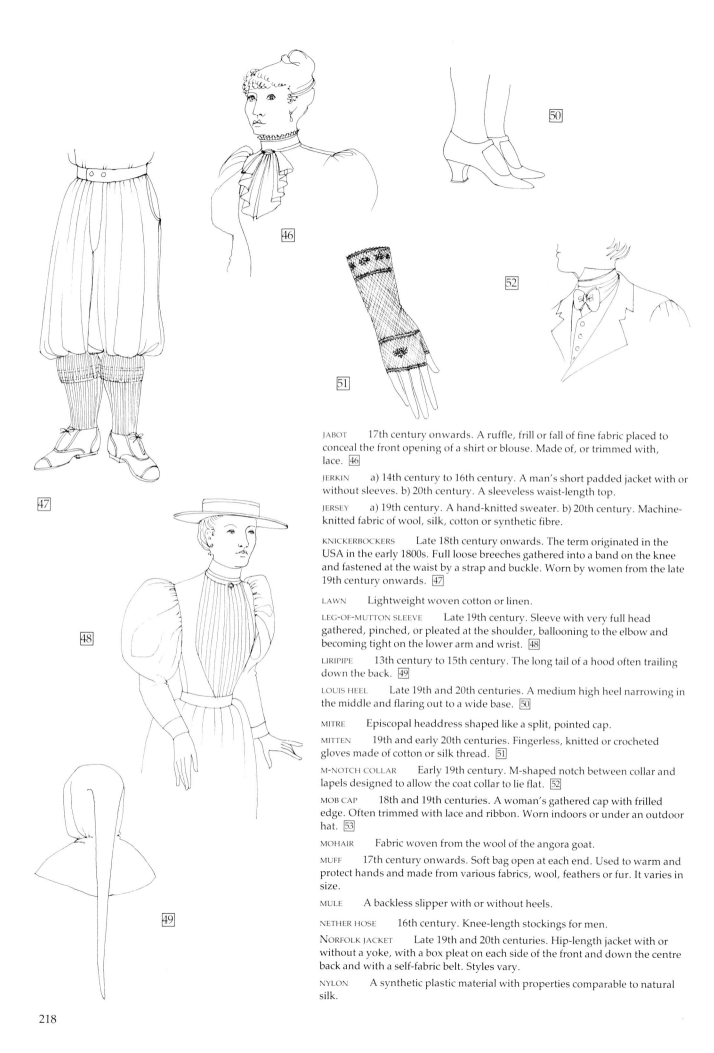

JABOT   17th century onwards. A ruffle, frill or fall of fine fabric placed to conceal the front opening of a shirt or blouse. Made of, or trimmed with, lace. 46

JERKIN   a) 14th century to 16th century. A man's short padded jacket with or without sleeves. b) 20th century. A sleeveless waist-length top.

JERSEY   a) 19th century. A hand-knitted sweater. b) 20th century. Machine-knitted fabric of wool, silk, cotton or synthetic fibre.

KNICKERBOCKERS   Late 18th century onwards. The term originated in the USA in the early 1800s. Full loose breeches gathered into a band on the knee and fastened at the waist by a strap and buckle. Worn by women from the late 19th century onwards. 47

LAWN   Lightweight woven cotton or linen.

LEG-OF-MUTTON SLEEVE   Late 19th century. Sleeve with very full head gathered, pinched, or pleated at the shoulder, ballooning to the elbow and becoming tight on the lower arm and wrist. 48

LIRIPIPE   13th century to 15th century. The long tail of a hood often trailing down the back. 49

LOUIS HEEL   Late 19th and 20th centuries. A medium high heel narrowing in the middle and flaring out to a wide base. 50

MITRE   Episcopal headdress shaped like a split, pointed cap.

MITTEN   19th and early 20th centuries. Fingerless, knitted or crocheted gloves made of cotton or silk thread. 51

M-NOTCH COLLAR   Early 19th century. M-shaped notch between collar and lapels designed to allow the coat collar to lie flat. 52

MOB CAP   18th and 19th centuries. A woman's gathered cap with frilled edge. Often trimmed with lace and ribbon. Worn indoors or under an outdoor hat. 53

MOHAIR   Fabric woven from the wool of the angora goat.

MUFF   17th century onwards. Soft bag open at each end. Used to warm and protect hands and made from various fabrics, wool, feathers or fur. It varies in size.

MULE   A backless slipper with or without heels.

NETHER HOSE   16th century. Knee-length stockings for men.

NORFOLK JACKET   Late 19th and 20th centuries. Hip-length jacket with or without a yoke, with a box pleat on each side of the front and down the centre back and with a self-fabric belt. Styles vary.

NYLON   A synthetic plastic material with properties comparable to natural silk.

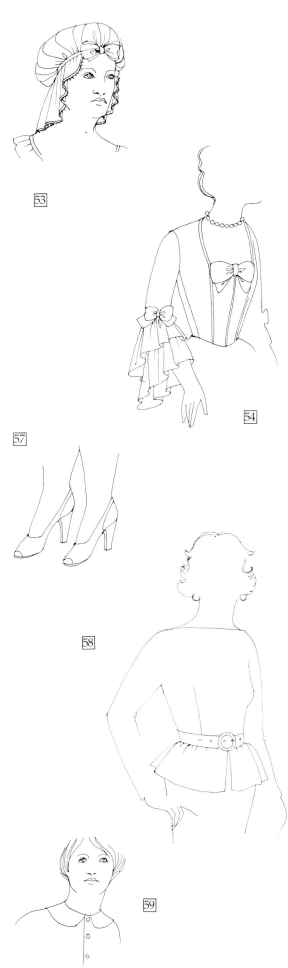

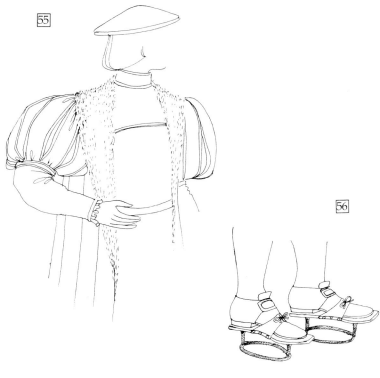

NYLONS   20th century. Stockings made from transparent nylon.

ORGANZA   A slightly stiffened, transparent, lightweight fabric, sometimes of silk, used for collars and cuffs etc. on women's garments.

PAGODA SLEEVE   18th century. A woman's sleeve fitted on the upper arm above the elbow. Frill from elbow to mid-arm at the front and to the wrist or lower at the back. 54

PANAMA HAT   19th and 20th centuries. Hat made from finely plaited straw. The crown has a raised centre crease and the brim can be turned up at the front or sides.

PANES   15th century to 17th century. Ribbon-like strips of fabric joined at the top and bottom to give the impression of a piece of slashed fabric. Lining fabrics or shirt sleeves would show through the slits. 55

PANNIER   17th and 18th centuries. A hoop of wicker. Originally funnel-shaped and later wide at the sides and flat in the front and back. Worn around the waist to support skirts and to give shape.

PARTI-COLOURED   14th and 15th centuries. A garment or part of a garment divided into different colours.

PATCH POCKET   Self-fabric sewn on to the outside of a garment with the top left open to serve as a pocket.

PATENT LEATHER   Early 19th century onwards. Lacquered leather used for evening pumps, slippers, shoes and bags.

PATTEN   14th century to mid-19th century. Shoe protector consisting of wooden sole with a leather strap over the foot. Raised above the ground on iron rings. 56

PEDAL PUSHERS   20th century. Mid-calf-length, tight-fitting trousers worn by women.

PEEP TOE   20th century. A shoe which has a section cut away at the front to reveal a toe or toes. 57

PELISSE   18th and 19th centuries. An outdoor coat or cape with or without sleeves. It comes in various lengths and is often fur-trimmed and fur-lined.

PEPLUM   A short flounce or overskirt attached to the hem of the bodice or belt. 58

PETER PAN COLLAR   Late 19th century onwards. A flat collar cut without a stand and with rounded edges. 59

PETTICOAT   a) 15th century to 18th century. An underskirt sewn to the gown. b) 19th and 20th centuries. An undergarment and support for heavy skirts.

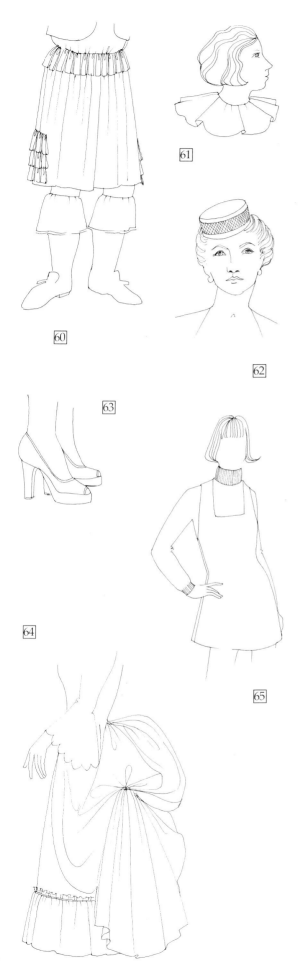

PETTICOAT BREECHES   17th century. Men's wide skirt-like breeches not gathered at the knee but decorated with ruffles, lace and ribbons. 60

PIERROT BODICE   18th century. A woman's tight-fitting bodice with full sleeves and deep peplum.

PIERROT COLLAR   20th century. A woman's circular-cut collar. 61

PILL-BOX HAT   A small, stiffened, round hat with straight sides and a flat top, worn mainly by women. 62

PLASTIC   A synthetic substance. Moulded into various forms as costume accessories and jewellery, and also as a textile.

PLATFORM SHOE   20th century. A shoe with a thick sole of cork, wood or plastic. 63

POLONAISE SKIRT   18th and 19th centuries. Skirts drawn up on cords into decorative swags or festoons to reveal an underskirt. 64

POLO NECK   20th century. A tube turned down over itself to form a double collar standing high into the neck. Mainly used in knitwear. 65

PRINCESS LINE   19th and 20th centuries. A woman's close-fitting garment cut in panels or gores without a waist seam. 66

PUFF SLEEVE   a) 15th century to 17th century. A puffed sleeve of various lengths, cut into horizontal sections and gathered into bands. b) 19th and 20th centuries. A short sleeve gathered into the armhole and into a band on the hem.

RAGLAN SLEEVE   18th century onwards. A sleeve which extends over the shoulder to the neckline. The sleeve itself is seamed under the arm. 67

RAYON   Man-made fibre woven into synthetic taffeta or crêpe de chine.

REDINGOTE   18th and 19th centuries. A woman's lightweight overcoat with fitted bodice and full skirt. Buttoned from the neck to the hem and often double-breasted. 68

REVERS   Also known as lapels. The facing is turned back to reveal the lining. Part of the bodice, jacket or coat. 69

ROSETTE   Ribbon pleated into a circular fan or looped into a circle, usually with a wide centre button. 70

ROULEAU   Bias-cut fabric sewn into a tube and used as a trimming or belt.

RUCHING   Finely pleated or gathered material.

RUFF   16th and 17th centuries. Circular collar of fine starched lawn, pleated and gathered in various ways. Sometimes open under the chin and often supported by a wire frame. 71

SACQUE   16th century to 18th century. Alternative spellings: sac, saque or, sack back. A woman's coat, jacket or gown with loose folds or pleats falling from the shoulders at the back to the hem. The front bodice, usually fitted to the waist, has a fine underskirt. [72]

SAFARI JACKET   20th century. Hip-length jacket made of lightweight fabric with collar and revers, shirt sleeves, large patch pockets, a waist-belt and, sometimes, a yoke.

SATIN   A closely woven silk fabric with a lustrous shine, particularly used for evening wear.

SCALLOPED   An edge cut in a series of semi-circular curves as a decorative effect.

SCAPULAR   Ecclesiastical garment consisting of a front and back hanging panel joined at the shoulders and open at the sides.

SELF-FABRIC   Garment detail or trimming, such as belts, patch pockets and bindings, in the same fabric as the body of the garment.

SEQUIN   A tiny, round, reflective disc with a central hole. Made from metal or plastic and used for decoration on evening wear and accessories.

SHAWL COLLAR   A continuous collar cut in one piece with the main body of the garment and incorporating both collar and revers. It has a seam at the centre back. [73]

SHIFT   A woman's simple sheath dress unstructured and unfitted, with or without sleeves and of various lengths. Used as an underdress, sleep wear or as a working dress.

SKULL CAP   A small, round, brimless cap worn on its own on the back of the head or as an undercap.

SLASH   15th century to 17th century. A slit or long hole cut or burned into the fabric of a garment to reveal the lining or undergarments.

SLING BACK   20th century. A woman's shoe exposed at the heel and held in place by a narrow strap.

SLIPPER   A low-cut shoe without fastenings or straps and into which the foot slips easily. [74]

SMOCKING   19th and 20th centuries. Closely pleated fabric held together by honeycomb needlework.

SNOOD   A hair net or openwork bag to hold the hair loosely at the back of the head. [75]

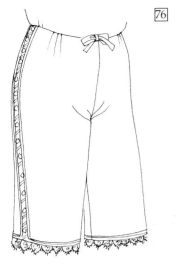

SPANISH BREECHES   16th and 17th centuries. Full, gathered breeches with high waist and long legs, worn by men. Left open at the knee and trimmed with ribbons. 76

SPAT   19th and 20th centuries. A man's ankle-length gaiter covering the upper of the shoe. Buttoned on the outside and fastened with a strap and buckle under the instep. Made from canvas or heavy felt. Usually white, grey or fawn. 77

SPENCER JACKET   18th and 19th centuries. A woman's short jacket with long tight sleeves for outdoor wear. Embroidered and sleeveless for indoor or evening wear. 78

SPUR   Metal spike strapped to the back of the heel. Used when riding.

STALK   A tuft or upturned stiffened tassel on a hat.

STAND COLLAR   19th and 20th centuries. Band of fabric standing high on the neck and covering the throat.

STAYS   17th century onwards. Also known as a corset. A two-piece fitted undergarment fastening both at the front and the back. Made from stiff canvas or boiled leather.

STILETTO HEEL   20th century, particularly 1950s. A woman's high narrow heel made from steel and coated with plastic. 79

STOCK   17th century onwards. A scarf, cravat or neck cloth tied around the neck and throat.

STOCK PIN   18th century onwards. Also known as a scarf pin, stick pin or cravat pin. An ornamental metal pin with a jewelled end used to hold the stock in place.

STOLE   A long, straight shoulder wrap. Made from most fabrics, feathers or furs. Can be knitted and often with fringed ends.

SUEDE   Undressed kid skin or leather with a velvet finish.

SURCOAT   9th century to 14th century. A loose outer garment drawn over the head. With or without sleeves and of varying lengths.

SURPLICE   Loose-fitting ecclesiastical vestment with wide sleeves. Usually made of white linen or lawn.

SWALLOWTAIL COAT   19th and 20th centuries. A man's coat with back skirts resembling the tails of a swallow. General term for men's formal evening attire.

SWEETHEART NECKLINE   A woman's neckline which is cut into two half-circles resembling a heart. 80

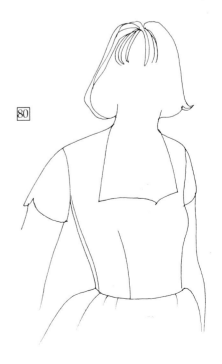

TAB a) 16th century. A small strip of ribbon sewn on to two open edges to act as a fastening. b) 17th century. A short, flat peplum piece sewn on to the hem of a doublet or bodice. 81

TABARD A short-sleeved or sleeveless tunic, sometimes open at the sides.

TAFFETA A rich silk fabric with a plain weave and a lustre. Used mainly for evening dresses.

TAILCOAT 19th and 20th centuries. Coat with backskirts only, cut into wide tails reaching to the knees.

TIARA A jewelled coronet worn by women, often without a back section.

TIPPET 14th century. A pendant fabric streamer attached to the upper arm and trailing to the ground.

TOP HAT 19th and 20th centuries. A tall, cylindrical, flat-topped hat with a narrow curving brim. 82

TRICORN HAT 18th century. Alternative spelling: tricorne. A hat with the brim caught up on three sides so as to form three points or horns. 83

TRILBY 19th and 20th centuries. Soft felt hat with a tall crown and a wide brim. Sometimes turned up on one side or at the back. 84

TRUNK HOSE 16th and 17th centuries. Short puffed breeches joined to stockings.

TURBAN A scarf or sash bound and twisted around the head in various ways.

TWEED A rough-textured, woven wool material often patterned with checks or stripes.

UPPER HOSE 15th century to 17th century. Long stockings reaching over the thigh to the waist.

VELVET A closely woven fabric with a short dense pile, the loops of which have usually been cut open. Made from silk, cotton or, now, from synthetic yarns.

VOILE A fine, plain, semi-transparent woven cloth made from silk, cotton, synthetic yarns or a mixture of fabrics.

WELT POCKET 19th and 20th centuries. A slit pocket bound on each side with the bindings overlapping. Used mainly on breast pockets on men's jackets.

WING COLLAR a) 16th century onwards. A woman's pointed collar cut in one piece with the bodice and turned upwards to stand against the back of the neck and away from the front. b) 19th and 20th centuries. A stiffened standing band worn by men. Open at the front and with the points turned down. 85

Bibliography

Anderson Black, J., and Madge Garland, *A History of Fashion*, 1975

Arnold, Janet, *Patterns of Fashion*, 1964

Battersby, Martin, *Art Deco Fashion*, 1974

Blum, Stella, *Victorian Fashions and Costumes*, 1974

————— (ed.), *Everyday Fashions of the Twenties*, 1981

Boucher, François, *A History of Costume in the West*, 1965; US title *20,000 Years of Fashion*

Bradfield, Nancy, *Historical Costumes of England*, 1958

Brook, Iris, *A History of English Costume*, 1937

Bruhn, Wolfgang, and Max Tilke, *A Pictorial History of Costume*, 1955

Byrne, Penelope, *The Male Image*, 1979

Contini, Mila, *Fashion*, 1965

Cunnington, C. W., and P., 'Handbook of English Costume' Series, 1952-1959

Cunnington, C. W., and P., and Charles Beard, *A Dictionary of English Costume*, 1960

Cunnington, Phillis, *Costume of Household Servants*, 1974

Cunnington, Phillis, and Catherine Lucas, *Occupational Costume in England*, 1967

Dorner, Jane, *Fashion in the Twenties and Thirties*, 1973

————— , *Fashion in the Forties and Fifties*, 1975

Drake, Nicholas, *The Fifties in Vogue*, 1987

Ewing, Elizabeth, *Fur in Dress*, 1981

Fowler, Kenneth, *The Age of the Plantagenet and Valois*, 1967

Gaunt, William, *Court Painting in England*, 1980

Gorsline, Douglas, *What People Wore*, 1978

Hall-Duncan, Nancy, *The History of Fashion Photography*, 1979

Hamilton-Hill, Margot, and Peter A. Bucknell, *The Evolution of Fashion 1066 to 1930*, 1967

Hansen, Henny Harald, *Costume Cavalcade*, 1956

Harrison, Michael, *The History of the Hat*, 1960

Hartley, Dorothy, *Medieval Costume and Life*, 1931

Herald, Jacqueline, *Renaissance Dress in Italy, 1400–1500*, 1981

Hermitage Museum, *The Art of Costume in Russia*, 1979

Holland, Vyvyan, *Hand Coloured Fashion Plates, 1770–1899*, 1988

Hopkins, J. C., *The Twentieth Century System of Ladies' Garment Cutting*, 1902

Houston, Mary G., *Medieval Costume in England and France*, 1939

Howell, Georgina, *In Vogue*, 1975

Kelsall, Freda, *How We Used to Live*, 1981

Kohler, Carl, *A History of Costume*, 1928

Langley-Moore, Doris, *Fashion through Fashion Plates*, 1971

Laver, James, *Costume Through the Ages*, 1961

————— , *Costume*, 1963

————— , *Costume and Fashion*, 1982

Lee-Potter, Charlie, *Sportswear in Vogue*, 1984

Lynam, Ruth, *Paris Fashion*, 1972

Mulvagh, Jane, *Vogue History of 20th Century Fashion*, 1988

O'Hara, Georgina, *The Encyclopaedia of Fashion*, 1986

Peacock, John, *Fashion Sketchbook, 1920–1960*, 1977

————— , *Costume 1066–1966*, 1986

Polhemus, Ted, and Lynn Proctor, *Fashion and Anti-Fashion*, 1978

Pringle, Margaret, *Dance Little Ladies*, 1977

Ribiero, Aileen, *Dress and Morality*, 1986

Sansom, William, *Victorian Life in Photographs*, 1974

Scott, Margaret, *Late Gothic Europe, 1400–1500*, 1980

Stevenson, Pauline, *Edwardian Fashion*, 1980

Strong, Roy, *The English Icon*, 1969

Waugh, Norah, *Corsets and Crinolines*, 1954

————— , *The Cut of Women's Clothes, 1600–1930*, 1968

Wilcox, R. Turner, *The Mode in Costume*, 1948

————— , *Five Centuries of American Costume*, 1963

Winter, Gordon, *A Country Camera, 1844–1914*, 1966

————— , *A Cockney Camera*, 1971

————— , *The Golden Years, 1903–1913*, 1975

Yarwood, Doreen, *English Costume*, 1951